WALKS FOR ALL SEASONS
DERBYSHIRE

Darley Park, Derby

WALKS FOR ALL SEASONS

DERBYSHIRE

Carol Burkinshaw

BRADWELL
BOOKS

Published by Bradwell Books
11 Orgreave Close Sheffield S13 9NP
Email: books@bradwellbooks.co.uk

British Library Cataloguing in Publication Data: a catalogue record for this book is available from the British Library.

1st Edition
ISBN: 9781912060528

Print: CPI Group (UK) Ltd, Croydon CR0 4YY
Design by: Andy Caffrey
Typesetting and mapping: Mark Titterton
Photograph credits: Carol Burkinshaw
Front cover: Karl Barton

Maps: Contain Ordnance Survey data
© Crown copyright and database right 2018
Ordnance Survey licence number 100039353

The information in this book has been produced in good faith and is intended as a general guide. Although the maps in this book are based on original Ordnance Survey (OS) mapping, walkers are always advised to use a detailed OS map. Look in 'The Basics' section for recommendations for the most suitable map for each of the walks.

Bradwell Books and the authors have made all reasonable efforts to ensure that the details are correct at the time of publication. Bradwell Books and the authors cannot accept responsibility for any changes that have taken place subsequent to the book being published.

It is the responsibility of individuals undertaking any of the walks listed in this book to exercise due care and consideration for their own health and well-being and that of others in their party. The walks in this book are not especially strenuous, but individuals taking part should ensure they are fit and well before setting off.

A good pair of walking books is essential for these walks. It is advisable to take good-quality waterproofs, and if undertaking the walks during the winter, take plenty of warm clothing as well. Because the walks will take some time, it would be a good idea to take along some food and drink. Enjoy walking. Enjoy Derbyshire with Bradwell Books!

CONTENTS

INTRODUCTION

I LOVE THE PEAK DISTRICT – YOU BET I DO – YET THERE'S A LOT MORE TO DERBYSHIRE THAN THE PRETTY FACE OF ITS DESERVEDLY POPULAR SLICE OF THE NATIONAL PARK. FOR ME, ITS GEOLOGICAL DARK AND WHITE PEAKS ARE THE TOP LAYER OF THE DERBYSHIRE CHOCOLATE BOX BUT, HIDDEN UNDERNEATH IT – TO ITS NORTH-EAST, EAST AND SOUTH – ARE LIP-SMACKING DELIGHTS JUST WAITING TO BE UNWRAPPED.

'Off Peak' Derbyshire is easy on both the eye and the legs. An understated beauty with a richly textured past that twenty family – and not forgetting pooch – friendly walks can only offer a taster of.

Its landscapes have powerful stories to tell and they don't get any bigger than in the Lower Derwent Valley where the 15-mile-long thread of the Derwent Valley Mills World Heritage Site spins a yarn of trailblazing entrepreneurs who gave birth to the modern factory system.

At Derby Silk Mill you'll meet John Lombe, who stitched together all the components of the manufacturing process to design the world's first factory. Alternatively, at Belper you can tread in the footsteps of Jedediah Strutt, a former financial partner of Richard Arkwright whose Matlock Bath/Cromford high-spec mills lie at the northern gateway of the World Heritage Site, as he set up his own textile empire and model community downstream.

INTRODUCTION

Other visionary front runners with strong connections to the county who helped unleash Britain's Industrial Revolution are the transport pioneers James Brindley and George Stephenson. Brindley's Trent and Mersey and Chesterfield canals were the key to unlock trading fortunes. Later in his railway career, Stephenson moved to Chesterfield to oversee the financial assets – coal and iron ore – he'd unearthed whilst tunnelling the Leeds–Derby railway.

Coal and iron ore were, of course, key ingredients fuelling Britain's industrialisation, both of which were found in abundance along Derbyshire's eastern side. Nowadays, it's difficult not to be 'ore' struck by the new face of mining and its associated transport corridors in the shape of country parks, nature reserves and off-road multi-user trails. Many of these 'green' shoots have matured into extensive leisure networks spanning the county border with Nottinghamshire, such as the Phoenix Greenways and the Erewash Trail.

Outside the national park the county is also well endowed with country estates offering the opportunity to peer into the lives of the often eccentric folk who lived there. Maybe wander around the Calke Abbey parklands, where behind closed doors generations of 'magpies' collected all sorts of things in a very 'unstately' house. Or admire the commanding presence of Bolsover Castle, which exudes drama from every angle for miles around. Built by the 1st Duke of Newcastle, it's a castle in name only, and presented a vast pleasure palace to lavishly entertain and curry favour, most notably with Charles I.

Bolsover Castle stands on a thin band of Magnesian limestone that runs from County Durham to Nottinghamshire, which is another geological feature that has provided inspiration for several walks, including the striking, yet little known, gorge at Pleasley Vale.

And just a twig snap from the Peak District, in places such as Ashover or Ashbourne you could be forgiven for thinking you were already in the origami peaks, as their underlying gritstone or limestone geology mirrors the national park's renowned Dark and White Peak areas.

But the subtle clue that you are in 'Off Peak' Derbyshire is that the crowds recede. So why not step off the well-tramped paths and explore the blissful countryside and timeless heritage that the rest of the county has to offer? It glitters in all seasons, and it seems that the weather is often much more agreeable to boot!

1 ASHBOURNE

Just like Ashbourne's traditional mass game of 'footy' – the annual Royal Shrovetide Football Match – this is a quirky ramble of two sides. The Georgian market town of Ashbourne versus the countryside charms of Mapleton, divided not by a river, but a long, former railway tunnel.

As it is a figure-of-eight walk, you can easily split this route into separate town and country outings, or you have the option to take the town centre element first or last.

With the eerie echo of an approaching train – if the sound system is playing – you head into Ashbourne's well-lit tunnel to emerge into the historic heart of the town where you'll find an excellent selection of independent shops. To your west, the tall spire of St Oswald's parish church pierces the skyline and to your east lies the Memorial Park, which was once part of the grounds of Ashbourne Hall.

For two days each year, since at least 1667, this bustling townscape is turned into a 'battlefield' as the Shrovetide Football game runs amok. Player numbers are unlimited, there are few rules and the goals are three miles apart. The teams consist of men, women and children of all ages, who represent the Up'ards or Down'ards depending on which side of Ashbourne's Henmore Brook they were born.

The ball is made of painted leather, weighs 4lbs and is filled with cork chippings so it floats in water. At 2pm on Shrove Tuesday and Ash Wednesday the ball is 'turned up' and play can go on until 10pm. In 1928, the then Prince of Wales (later Edward VIII) 'turned up' the ball, earning the game its 'royal' title, and in 2003 the current Prince of Wales (Charles) repeated this honour.

Returning to your start point, via the tunnel, you join the Tissington Trail, which tracks the ex-Ashbourne to Buxton branch line for 13 miles to Parsley Hay where it joins the High Peak Trail.

Departing the trail, undulating fields and woodland lead you to the tranquil red-brick village of Mapleton clustered around its tiny, domed church and the Okeover Arms. Rising behind Mapleton there are attractive views across the village on the east bank of the Dove to the Okeover estate on the Staffordshire side of the river. The conical-shaped 'mini mountain' of Thorpe Cloud, at the southern gateway to Dovedale, adds a dramatic dimension to the scene.

THE BASICS

Distance: 5¾ miles / 9.5km

Gradient: Level walking through Ashbourne town centre and along the multi-user Tissington Trail. The balance of the walk is undulating.

Severity: Moderate

Approx. time to walk: 3 hours

Stiles: Eight

Maps: OS Landranger 119 (Buxton & Matlock); OS Explorer 259 (Derby)

Path description: Urban/parkland in Ashbourne, Tissington Trail and rolling field paths. The latter are prone to seasonal mud.

Start point: Tissington Trail car park, Mapleton Lane, on the outskirts of Ashbourne (GR SK 175469)

Parking: Tissington Trail car park, Mapleton Lane, on the outskirts of Ashbourne (DE6 1FD)

Dog friendly: Yes, but there are a number of stiles and leads will be required around livestock

Public toilets: Tissington Trail car park at start point and Ashbourne town centre (signed)

Nearest food: Light refreshments at Tissington Trail car park, various in Ashbourne town centre and the Okeover Arms at Mapleton

1 ASHBOURNE WALK

Route

1. Head south from the car park through the Ashbourne Tunnel. Exit the tunnel and turn left onto Station Road. Go left over Henmore Brook and at a T-junction turn left onto Church Street. After circling around the parish church, walk back along Church Street and maintain direction onto St John's Street to the gallows-style inn sign. Suspended across the full width of the street, this unusual sign resulted from the amalgamation of two coaching inns – the Green Man and Black's Head.

2. Bear left up Victoria Square to the marketplace, cross the road and turn right down to St John Street. Go left to Madge's Corner and pass through a gate to the side of the War Memorial Gates into the Memorial Park. Follow the path along the right-hand perimeter of the park to a lake. Loop around the lake and retrace your route through the park to St John's Street. Proceed along this street, passing Ashbourne's famed gingerbread shop, and walk back under the gallows sign. Return to your start point by turning left onto Station Road and picking up the tunnel again on your right.

3. Beyond the car park and cycle hire centre, link into the Tissington Trail. Cross a watercourse and a road bridge and then after passing Redhouse Farm on your left, look out for a path crossing the trail by a public footpath sign.

4. Turn left through a gate into a field. Ascend the field to the left of a tree to another gate. Cross the middle of the next field – your first viewpoint of Thorpe Cloud is to the right – to a signpost onto Spend Lane.

5. Walk left, and then in a few yards turn right along the driveway of Ash Dove to a signpost in 15 yards. Veer half-left to the rear of houses to a large waymarked gate. Cross a small field to a stile. Walk half-right across the next field to a stile in a corner by a fenced-off plantation. Immediately go over a wooden plank bridge and divert right, sticking close to the field edge, to a gate.

6. Go left through the gate to descend into Hinchley Wood. At a marker post branch left and then keep ahead at a second marker post to exit the woodland. Maintain direction across a field to a gate where you have a pleasing outlook over Mapleton and into Staffordshire. Walk diagonally right to climb a stile near a field corner.

7. Continue ahead by a hedge and when it ends veer right to the rear of Mapleton's churchyard. At the far side of the church grounds negotiate a gate and head past the church to a lane.

8. Turn left and after the Okeover Arms, go left at a signpost for Ashbourne. Cross a stile, ascend for 30 yards, and then swing right to climb more gently past redundant stiles to a marker post. Turn left across two fields and then go over a wooden plank bridge and stile. Follow an enclosed path over a track – signed Ashbourne – passing a campsite and continue forwards, descending fields via stiles to the Tissington Trail. Turn right to return to the car park.

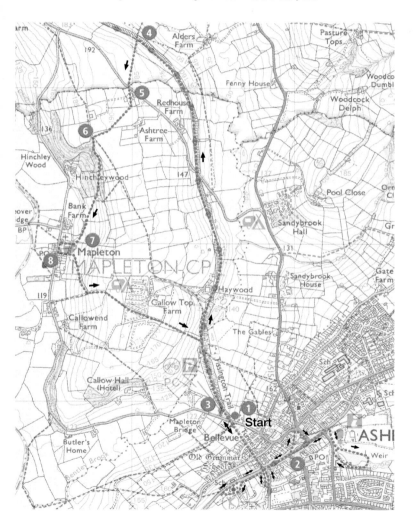

2 ASHOVER

IF YOU'RE LOOKING FOR A GREAT PUB WALK, COMPLEMENTED BY A HISTORIC VILLAGE THAT LOOKS AS THOUGH IT HAS BEEN AIRLIFTED, ALONG WITH THE SURROUNDING SCENERY, FROM THE PEAK DISTRICT, THEN THIS ONE IS FOR YOU!

Ashover, meaning 'ridge where ash trees grow', lies in the Amber Valley. It's home to three thriving inns and full of rural community spirit, so you can afford to work up a thirst on this rolling figure-of-eight walk, where the two loops conveniently meet at another delightful hostelry at Milltown.

Ashover's 15th-century Crispin Inn, however, received unwelcome drinkers during the English Civil War when Royalists, already having swigged the cellars dry at nearby Eddlestow Hall while the owner was absent, forcibly removed the landlord from his alehouse and either drank or poured its brew away.

Sadly, Cromwell's Parliamentarians also paid Ashover an unpleasant visit as, short of ammunition, they ransacked its church for lead to make bullets and reduced neighbouring Eastwood Hall to ruins.

One of the delights of Ashover's lovely parish church, with its tall slender spire that dominates the landscape for miles around, is its lead font, which was saved from the looting Roundheads by the quick-thinking vicar performing an unexpected burial. It's the only lead font to survive in Derbyshire, which is surprising for a county once renowned for its lead mining.

Leaving Ashover you soon gain height, and vistas along the Amber Valley, to reach Overton Hall. This was once home to the famous botanist Sir Joseph Banks, who accompanied Captain James Cook on his first voyage of discovery to the South Pacific in the late 1760s.

A wander through the hall's estate guides you to the tiny hamlet of Milltown and the Miners Arms Inn. A high-level traverse, offering fine views, later descends to Ogston Reservoir. This dam is operated by Severn Trent Water as a holding ground for Carsington Water (Walk 6). It's also home to one of Britain's largest bird clubs and the popular Ogston Sailing Club.

It was on this body of water that Dame Ellen MacArthur learnt to handle her craft before she went on to sail into the record books in 2005 by setting the world's fastest time to date for a solo circumnavigation of the globe.

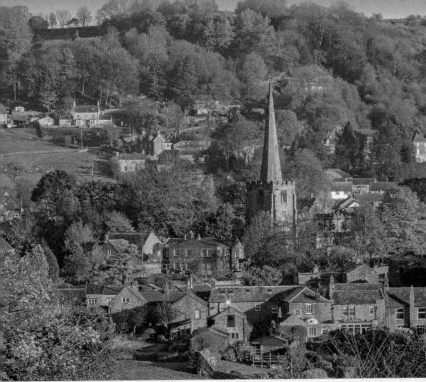

THE BASICS

Distance: 5¾ miles / 9.5km

Gradient: Rises and falls throughout, although after the initial stiffish climb it's not particularly demanding – take your time and enjoy the views

Severity: Moderate

Approx. time to walk: 3 hours

Stiles: Three

Maps: OS Landranger 269 (Chesterfield & Alfreton); OS Explorer 119 (Buxton & Matlock)

Path description: Field and woodland paths and quiet lanes

Start point: Car park at Ashover Parish Hall on Milken Lane (GR SK 351632)

Parking: Car park at Ashover Parish Hall on Milken Lane (S45 0AD)

Dog friendly: Yes, but on leads along lanes and around livestock

Public toilets: Ashover, close to start (signed from Black Swan along Moor Lane)

Nearest food: Three pubs in Ashover and light refreshments at the village's Ye Old Tuckshop. Miners Arms Inn at Milltown.

2 ASHOVER WALK

ROUTE

1. Exit the car park left onto Milken Lane and go left at the junction adjacent to the Black Swan, passing the Crispin Inn and parish church. At the next road junction, in front of the Old Poets' Corner pub, walk left for a few yards and turn right onto the signed bridleway. Descend to the Amber, bend left and right, and then ascend, ignoring offshoots, to a wide T-junction. Walk left to a path intersection in 40 yards with a lovely panorama back over Ashover.

2. Turn right and at the next crossroads head left through the Overton estate. Maintain direction along Gin Lane, passing a pond, with the crags of Cocking Tor to your right. On meeting a track bear left, and when this trackway swerves right, stick ahead on a signed public footpath. After dropping down several steps, veer  right on an unsigned path and go right at a T-junction to emerge onto a lane at Milltown next to the Miners Arms.

3. Turn right along the lane and take the second road on your left – The Hay. This lane ascends and later curves left to pass an old chapel and then descends to a T-junction. Walk right to the B6014.

4. Bear left along the road and in 50 yards turn right through a gate. Immediately branch left at a fork – with Ogston Reservoir now in sight – to follow the bridleway along a right-hand field edge. Negotiate a gate onto an enclosed path and keep ahead to a lane. Turn left towards Ogston Reservoir.

5. At a T-junction – Ogston Sailing Club and Ogston Reservoir's west car park with picnic tables are just to the right – your route is left. After passing the one-time Woolley Methodist Chapel, you reach a junction. Turn left – or right for 50 yards for fine prospect across the reservoir – for a few yards and divert right at a signpost.

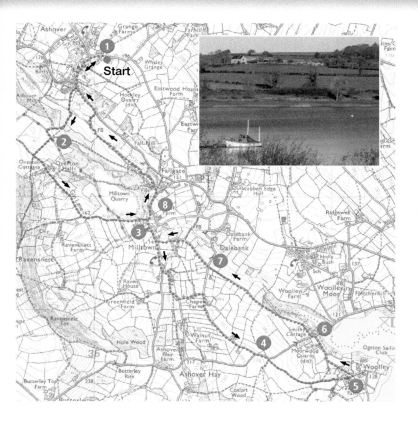

6. Walk along two right-hand field boundaries and climb a stile into woodland. Follow the path above the Amber and exit the trees over another stile. Keep ahead over a third stile and then look out for a small gate on your left. Continue along a track to a reach a road junction.

7. Join Brown Lane opposite and turn right at a T-junction to retrace your steps to the Miners Arms Inn at Milltown. Just after the pub, the lane bends left onto Fallgate beside the Amber. Shortly after passing a weir, cross a footbridge – signed 'footpath' – and go right along the riverbank to a lane at the hamlet of Fallgate.

8. Turn left along the signed bridleway and veer right when the path splits at Demonsdale Farm. Pass through a gate and follow the Amber over a clapper bridge. The path then heads away from the river up to a lane, and you walk left back into Ashover. Turn right at the Old Poets' Corner and right again at the Black Swan back to the village hall.

3 BELPER

'STRUTT' YOUR STUFF AMID THE MILLS AND HILLS OF BELPER AT THE HEART OF THE DERWENT VALLEY MILLS WORLD HERITAGE SITE, WHICH, WITHIN A 15-MILE STRETCH FROM ITS NORTHERN GATEWAY AT MATLOCK BATH TO THE CITY OF DERBY, WITNESSED THE BIRTH OF THE MODERN FACTORY SYSTEM.

Jedediah Strutt made his initial fortune with his invention of the Derby Rib, an attachment to a framework knitting machine that could produce ribbed stockings. This enabled him to financially partner Richard Arkwright in creating the first mass-production factory and model village at Matlock Bath/Cromford, which motivated Strutt to invest in his own textile dynasty downstream at Belper/Milford.

Like many early timber-framed mills, Strutt's original Belper North Mill was destroyed by fire, but Strutt's son, William, quickly rebuilt it with a 'fire-resistant' iron frame that revolutionised global construction design. Today Strutt's North Mill museum, which incorporates the Derwent Valley visitor centre, weaves the transformation of Belper from a hamlet of nail makers to a flourishing town acclaimed by Georgian fashion icons for its daring stockings.

The best way to appreciate the innovative and paternalistic influence of generations of Strutts on Belper is on foot. From the North Mill, you cross Belper Bridge to the viewing area over the magnificent Horseshoe Weir against the backdrop of the North and East mills. On the opposite side of the road you can explore the tiny Beaurepaire Gardens – the town's name is derived from a word meaning 'beautiful retreat'.

Heading back across the Derwent you go under a footbridge that linked the North Mill to the one-time West Mill. The openings along the bridge to site guns were designed to discourage Luddites from causing 'trouble at t'mill'. Next on your left is the imposing red-brick East Mill. This isn't a Strutt legacy as it was built in 1912 by the English Sewing Company.

On the other side of the A6 you get a feel for the high-quality housing the Strutts provided for their millworkers along the terraced cobbles of Long Row and its parallel streets of clusters – blocks of semi-detached, back-to-back houses – named after Jedediah's three sons, William, George and Joseph. You'll see examples of community facilities provided in the shape of a school and churches and be surprised by the Leeds–Derby railway line that the acclaimed railway engineer George Stephenson literally scythed through the town, requiring eleven bridges along one mile of track. And on Joseph Street there's a rare early 19th-century nail shop.

After exploring the War Memorial Gardens and the Market Place you enter Belper Parks. Once part of the deer parks of Duffield Frith and now a local nature reserve, the park's mixed habitats deliver views across the Derwent Valley to the Chevin ridge.

From this haven you head back through the town centre to relax in the River Gardens. This was an early 20th-century gift presented by the Strutts to Belper, which with its well-tended flower displays, water features and bandstand is a gorgeous spot to picnic or hire a rowing boat in the summer.

THE BASICS

Distance: 2½ miles / 4km

Gradient: Gently undulating

Severity: Easy

Approx. time to walk: 1½ hours

Stiles: None

Maps: OS Landranger 119 (Buxton & Matlock); OS Explorer 259 (Derby)

Path description: Town and parkland

Start point: Belper River Gardens car park, off the A6 at the rear of the town's East Mill (GR SK 346481)

Parking: Belper River Gardens car park, off the A6 at the rear of the town's East Mill (DE56 1BE), or alternatively the Coppice car park (free) accessed from Belper's Market Place

Dog friendly: Yes, but on a lead for the town section

Public toilets: Belper River Gardens car park

Nearest food: Various in Belper

ROUTE

1. From the rear of the car park, beyond the toilet facilities, follow the path to the front of Strutt's North Mill. Turn right onto the road and cross the Derwent to a viewing area by the water's edge. On the opposite side of the road is the Beaurepaire Gardens. Retrace your steps back over the river and under an archway to the A6. The East Mill is to your left.

2. Using the pedestrian crossing go over the A6 and turn right. In 30 yards turn left along the cobbles of Long Row. Part way up the hill is the railway that was cut through Belper and an information board. When the cobbles end, curve right onto Green Lane. The next three streets on your right – William, George and Joseph – were named after Strutt's three sons. Thirty yards along Joseph Street is an old nail shop. On your left are three churches in quick succession – the Unitarian Chapel, the Congregational Church and St Peter's, which are all worth a short detour.

3. At the T-junction with King Street the War Memorial Gardens facing you are again of interest. Go left to the Market Place. A pedestrian crossing leads you to the market cross where you bear right into the signed Coppice car park.

4. From the information board in the Coppice car park drop down steps and go over Coppice Brook. At the fork immediately in front of you bear left to gently ascend, ignoring all offshoots, through woodland to reach a large junction with a tree in the middle of it. Walk right and stick to the main path ahead to a Belper Parks information board close to housing.

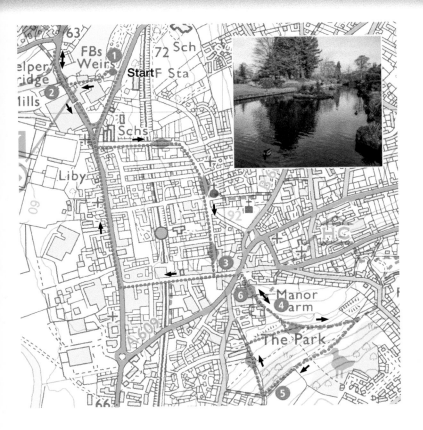

5. Branch right and at a crossroads by a marker post turn right. In 2014, near the top of the far side of the Derwent Valley, Belper's army cadets planted 25 million poppy seeds spelling out 'WW1' to commemorate the 100th anniversary of the start of the conflict. Keep ahead at a junction – marked Derwent Valley Heritage Way – and descend steps to a football pitch. At the far side of the pitch, look out for a marker post over to the right, and take the second of two right-hand paths. Underneath overhead wires veer left to negotiate Coppice Brook at the same point as in route instruction 4 and head back up to the Coppice car park.

6. Exit the car park into the Market Place and cross the road to return to King Street. Follow this road to the A6 and turn right along the pavement, which leads you to the River Gardens car park behind East Mill. You can explore the gardens beyond the car park at your leisure.

4 BOLSOVER

OVERLOOKING THE VALE OF SCARSDALE AND VISIBLE FOR MILES AROUND, BOLSOVER'S FAIRY-TALE CASTLE, CROWNING THE SPUR OF A MAGNESIAN LIMESTONE ESCARPMENT, WAS CONSTRUCTED NOT FOR MILITARY PURPOSES BUT TO TURN POWERFUL HEADS.

Although it was the busy Norman castle builders who first spotted the site's defensive potential, today's 'fortress' was built by the son, Charles Cavendish, and grandson, William Cavendish, of the formidable Bess of Hardwick from nearby Hardwick Hall.

William's principal seat was just across the Nottinghamshire border at Welbeck Abbey and his fantasy keep-like 'Little Castle' of stately rooms and its accompanying enormous terrace range regally entertained Charles I on several occasions. For his staunch Royalist support during the Civil War, William was later created 1st Duke of Newcastle. And as a flamboyant playboy and skilled horseman he added a Riding House complex to the castle grounds that went on to become the model for modern dressage arenas.

From Bolsover's town centre you join the Back Hills that run just below the limestone ridgetop. On a clear day to the south you may pick out Hardwick Hall on the skyline, and on the opposite side of the M1 stands the evocative shell of Sutton Scarsdale Hall.

In the foreground is the country's first mining village created on 'garden city' lines during the late 19th century by the Bolsover Colliery Company. You head down to New Bolsover, which stands quite separately from the main town on the Doe Lea valley floor and link into the Peter Fidler nature reserve.

This wildlife habitat occupies an old colliery spoil heap and is dedicated to the explorer Peter Fidler who was born at Mill Farm in 1769 on the doorstep of the later coalmine. History has cruelly forgotten Peter, but his intrepid achievement of opening up western Canada through his exploration and mapping is immense. After visiting a cairn, similar to a memorial to Peter in Dauphin, Canada, you link into the Carr Vale nature reserve via the multi-user Stockley Trail.

A longish climb then leads you back up to the ridgetop at Palterton, where you are rewarded with fine views as you head towards to Bolsover. The final stretch follows a medieval town embankment as it curves through Bolsover's Hornscroft Park.

THE BASICS

Distance: 5½ miles / 9km

Gradient: One descent near the start and a long gradual incline up Carr Lane to Palterton

Severity: Moderate

Approx. time to walk: 2¾ hours

Stiles: None

Maps: OS Landranger 120 (Mansfield & Worksop); OS Explorer 269 (Chesterfield & Alfreton)

Path description: A good nature reserve path network, fields, lanes and a multi-user trail

Start point: Town End car park off the A632 near Bolsover's Market Place, or any other public car park near Bolsover Castle (GR SK 474705)

Parking: Town End car park off the A632 near Bolsover's Market Place, or any other public car park near Bolsover Castle (S44 6DB). Alternatively, there is a car park for the Stockley Trail at the end of Riverside Way, off the A632 (S44 6GA).

Dog friendly: Yes, but on leads along roads and in the Peter Fidler and Carr Vale nature reserves

Public toilets: None

Nearest food: Various pubs and cafes in Bolsover, and Castle Arms at bottom of Bolsover Hill on the A632

4 BOLSOVER WALK

ROUTE

1. Exit the car park onto the A632. Turn right and in several yards go over a pedestrian crossing into the Market Place. Bear right and then left, signed for Bolsover Castle. The road veers left by the castle entrance and swings left again onto High Street to reach the parish church at a junction. At the far side of the petrol station opposite the church, turn right onto a signed path and shortly curve right along Bolsover's Back Hills. Descend steps and maintain direction at a junction to Castle Lane, where a conduit house that once supplied water to Bolsover Castle can be seen.

2. Cross the lane and descend to a bend. Go right onto a signed public footpath and emerge into the open below Bolsover Castle at a marker post. Walk downhill along the edge of Castle Fields to another marker post.

3. Bear left for 20 yards along a track and then branch right to the edge of the New Bolsover colliery village. When the path splits again, walk half-right across grass and stick ahead along a road with the colliery village sports facilities to your left.

4. Just before reaching the A632 pass through a gate on your left into a field and head half-right to the A road. Cross over with care and walk left to a roundabout. Immediately after Riverside Way on your left – brown sign for Stockley Trail car park – pass through an A-frame to a T-junction. Go right into the Peter Fidler nature reserve and veer left at a path intersection to a cairn dedicated to the man after whom the reserve is named.

5. After the cairn, fork right to a junction in-between a bench and a pond. Turn right and then at a T-junction at the edge of the reserve go left. Walk left again at the next path intersection and ascend to two benches with a fine elevated view over Carr Vale nature reserve and Sutton Scarsdale  Hall. The path later bends left by a series of information boards and descends to the Stockley Trail and a sculpture called Breaking the Mould.

6. Walk right along the trail and when a track crosses the trail, turn right into the Carr Vale nature reserve by an information board. Cross the River Doe Lea and turn immediately left to walk alongside the reserve's ponds. Just before the end of the last lake go back over the river and cross the Stockley Trail via A-frames to pass a secluded fishing pond.

7. Continue along a surfaced track and when it bends to the left, go right at a public footpath sign along a field edge. The path curves first left to become a track and then right at a junction to reach a lane.

8. Go left to gradually climb Carr Lane to the edge of Palterton. Go left at a signpost along a cottage-lined track. Pass through a gate into a field and head over to its far right-hand corner. Stick ahead towards Bolsover and negotiate a gate to walk in-between houses to the A632.

9. Cross over and turn left. After a cemetery enter Hornscroft Park to follow its curling embankment – in the centre of the park the former bowling green has been sculptured into 'the Bowl' – to a crossroads with traffic lights. Utilising a pedestrian crossing, maintain direction back into Bolsover's town centre.

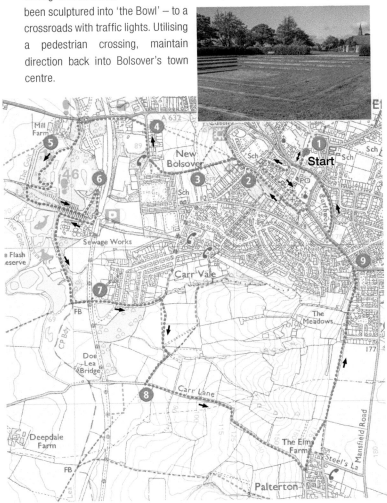

5 CALKE ABBEY

DIP YOUR TOES INTO A WATERY AND HISTORICAL EXTRAVAGANZA STRADDLING THE DERBYSHIRE AND LEICESTERSHIRE BORDERS, WHICH EXPLORES TWO CONTRASTING COUNTRY HOUSE ESTATES AND OFFERS AN INTRIGUING INSIGHT INTO THE STORIES THEY HAVE TO TELL.

Calke Abbey, never actually the site of an abbey, but a medieval priory, was the country pile of the Harpur-Crewe family from 1622 to 1985. It then came into the hands of the National Trust, who discovered they'd been handed the key to an Aladdin's cave that provided a unique record of the eccentric lives of Calke Abbey's upper-crust owners.

As the family cut themselves off from society, the vast and rambling Calke Abbey had become home to generations of compulsive collectors and hoarders. So not only did the National Trust find the structure of the house in a terrible condition, but every nook and cranny was cluttered with 'stuff'. It was a dusty cabinet of curiosities crammed with both significant natural history collections and everyday objects that were piled high in long-abandoned rooms. And the remaining rooms that were lived in could at best be described as decidedly 'unstately'.

One of the treasures that came to light was a Chinese state bed, complete with silk hangings, that a daughter of George II had given to the 5th Baronet Harpur as a wedding present. It had never been removed from its packing case.

Rather than restore the interior of Calke to its former glory the National Trust took the decision to preserve it as they found it as a symbolic representation of the faded glory of so many country houses that slid down the 20th-century property ladder.

Next to Calke is the hamlet of Staunton Harold, which sits tucked just inside Leicestershire and for 500 years became the focal point of the Shirley family's estate. Their family fortunes were a bit like the game of snakes and ladders. When Oliver Cromwell became Lord Protector of England the staunchly Royalist Sir Robert Shirley, with cavalier disregard for Cromwell's Puritanism, built a church at Staunton Harold. This disobedience led to his early death aged 27 in the Tower of London.

During the later reign of Queen Anne, the Shirleys became the Earls Ferrers. The rakish 4th Earl was convicted of murdering his steward, which earned him the dubious distinction of being the last peer in Britain to be hanged. Following the national pattern of decline, the 12th Earl put Staunton Hall up for sale in 1954, but in 2003 it once again became a family home, idyllically located next to Robert Shirley's church and the estate lakes. Behind the hall, the former stable block is now the Ferrers Centre for Arts and Crafts.

From the southern end of Staunton Harold Reservoir, which was created from one of Calke Abbey's ponds, you enter Dimminsdale Nature Reserve. Like the dam, the nature reserve is owned by Severn Trent Water, but the latter is managed by Leicestershire and Rutland Wildlife Trust. During the 18th and 19th centuries, this wildlife haven, known for its great swathes of snowdrops, was mined for limestone and lead. When the mineral extraction ceased the quarries were flooded to form pools and brooks resulting in a good mix of habitats.

You then visit the delightful hamlet of Staunton Harold and wind your way through the grounds of Calke Abbey before the final stretch along the shoreline of Staunton Harold Reservoir.

THE BASICS

Distance: 5 miles / 8km

Gradient: One short ascent and two descents, otherwise easy going

Severity: Moderate

Approx. time to walk: 2½ hours

Stiles: Four

Maps: OS Landranger 128 (Derby & Burton upon Trent); OS Explorer 245 (National Forest)

Path description: Good estate and field paths and quiet lanes

Start point: Round car park at the southern end of Staunton Harold Reservoir (GR SK 375226)

Parking: Round car park at the southern end of Staunton Harold Reservoir (LE65 1RR)

Dog friendly: Yes, but on leads around livestock and Dimminsdale Nature Reserve

Public toilets: Ferrers Centre at Staunton Harold

Nearest food: Ferrers Centre and Nurseries at Staunton Harold

5 CALKE ABBEY WALK

ROUTE

1. Exit the car park and follow the quiet lane to a T-junction and turn left. In several hundred yards look out for an information board on your right for Dimminsdale Nature Reserve. Head into its woodland and turn right in front of a lake. Pass more pools and curve left over a brook to a yellow footpath marker. Go right to meet a driveway on the Staunton Harold estate.

2. Divert left along the estate road to a junction and branch left to explore the lovely Staunton Harold hamlet. When you're ready, return to this junction and turn left. In 50 yards, when the driveway bends left, negotiate a gate on your right by a signpost. Head for the far left-hand corner of the field and then follow yellow-topped marker posts across several fields and a brook to a lane at Heath End. Turn right and at a T-junction go left.

3. In 100 yards climb a stile on your right and track the field edges over several stiles to a lane. Turn right to enter the Calke Abbey estate along a surfaced lane. Keep ahead on meeting a driveway coming in from your left and when Calke Abbey comes into view watch out carefully for yellow waymarkers around a tree before the brow of the hill.

4. Turn left at the tree. At first the path is indistinct, but in 100 yards pick up a grassy path in-between a line of trees that soon begins to drop downhill. Ignore all offshoots and nearing a pond veer right to a gate to emerge in between two ponds. Walk right, initially above the pond, and at a path intersection fork left to hug the water's edge. At the end of the lake the path bends left uphill.

5. At the top of the rise walk right and follow this track as it swerves right and descends to Staunton Harold reservoir. Cross the weir and swing first left and then right back up to the car park.

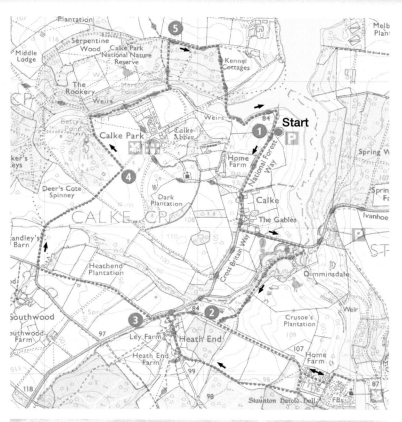

6 CARSINGTON WATER

As a significant pool in our water supply and a deservedly popular recreational playground for all the family, the huge expanse of Carsington Water works hard and plays hard.

It takes its name from the nearby ancient village of Carsington, but the outlook that the Roman lead miners would have had of their surroundings would have been somewhat different to today. They also missed out on a lakeside holiday retreat and an opportunity to meet the Queen when she officially opened England's ninth-largest reservoir in 1992!

Ramblers and cyclists circumnavigate the eight-mile-long trail around the reservoir. For the more adventurous, the watersports centre and sailing club open up a whole raft of other attractions. In addition, the large visitor centre offers an interactive exhibition that's all about H_2O, shops and refreshment facilities that may be enjoyed with a balcony bird's-eye view over this hive of human and wildlife activity.

Yet the construction of the reservoir was far from plain sailing. After years of controversy running from the 1960s, Carsington Water was finally given the go-ahead in 1980, but in 1984, when the project was almost complete, disaster struck and the dam collapsed. Work on a new design was finally agreed in 1989 and so the reservoir was actually twelve years in the making.

Owned and operated by Severn Trent Water, Carsington Water is a credit to them. Not only are they managing a major tourist attraction and wildlife haven, they balance this with the reservoir providing water day to day to three million people in local counties. Carsington also has the strategic capability during drought conditions to top up the Severn Trent grid system at the outer reaches of its organisational compass points.

Your walk begins with a short circuit of Stones Island, which is attached to the mainland. You can, of course, save this to the end of your walk, or strip it out altogether, but it offers an interesting 'inside out' perspective on Carsington Water's setting. The 'island' represents Severn Trent's contribution to the Derbyshire tradition of building hilltop monuments, as at its summit is a sculpture of stones cut from the Dark Peak's millstone grit. Each stone varies in size and has a strategic hole punched through it designed to focus your attention on a particular point in the landscape.

You then amble across the top of the dam wall to the control tower that operates as the 'tap' to turn on or off the flow of water between the River Derwent, which supplies most of Carsington's water, and the reservoir. Next to the tower is a large viewing area. The return leg follows quiet, scenic tracks below the gigantic dam wall where you get another opportunity to appreciate the sheer scale of Carsington Water from a different angle.

THE BASICS

Distance: 3¾ miles / 6km

Gradient: Gently undulating away from the reservoir shoreline, otherwise easy going

Severity: Moderate

Approx. time to walk: 2 hours

Stiles: None

Maps: OS Landranger 119 (Buxton & Matlock); OS Explorer OL24 The Peak District (White Peak area)

Path description: Good path network maintained by Severn Trent Water with some seasonal mud away from the reservoir shoreline

Start point: Carsington Water visitor centre, off the B5035 (GR SK 241516)

Parking: Carsington Water visitor centre, off the B5035 (DE6 1ST)

Dog friendly: Yes, but signs request dogs to be on leads at all times

Public toilets: Carsington Water visitor centre, or just off route at Carsington Water's Millfields car park

Nearest food: Carsington Water visitor centre restaurant and cafe, or just off route light refreshments are available at Carsington Water's Millfields car park

6 CARSINGTON WATER WALK

ROUTE

1. From the signpost in-between the visitor centre and watersports centre, head in the direction of Stones Island. A surfaced path circles this tiny 'island', but there are many offshoots that you can pick and choose from to get closer to the shore – heed the signs for soft mud – for the best views and picnic benches before returning to your start point.

2. Go left in front of the visitor centre and at a signpost in 50 yards branch left – signed Dam Wall and Millfields. Cross a road at the entrance to Carsington Sailing Club and in 10 yards turn left to walk between the sailing club and a road. Maintain direction at a junction, which you will return to later, to follow the dam wall.

3. Shortly after passing the Water Drawing Tower, bear left into a large viewing area and follow its edge to a path intersection. The Millfields car park and its facilities, including picnic benches, are a short distance to your left, but you go forwards for 10 yards, turn right and divert left at a signpost in 30 yards.

4. Cross a road and pick up the surfaced downhill lane opposite. When the lane ends, join a path, which curves right to cross a track and then a bridge next to a ford. Go through a gate and wind your way along a gently ascending grassy track – ignore any offshoots – close to the reservoir embankment. Later the track swings left to a Visitor Centre signpost and you follow its uphill direction to negotiate a gate. In 50 yards the track bends right, with views of Hognaston village to your left, and then right again with Carsington Water ahead.

5. Cross a road and walk left to retrace your steps back to the visitor centre, by turning right across the entrance to the sailing club and following the path ahead back to the visitor centre.

7 CHESTERFIELD

Build up a head of steam and discover how the pioneering innovators – James Brindley and George Stephenson – transported Chesterfield into the Industrial Revolution. And be 'inspired' by the twist in the tale of Chesterfield's landmark crooked spire.

Chesterfield began life as a Roman fort, but it wasn't until the 46-mile-long Chesterfield Canal opened up a vital 'highway' to the North Sea via the Trent and Humber in 1777 that the market town arrived on the map.

Although he didn't survive to see the waterway operational its engineer was the national guru of cutting-edge canal technology, James Brindley. His bold design for the canal incorporated several double, treble and even quadruple locks, plus a 2,880-yard (2,633m) tunnel. The boats, pulled by horses, which carried the canal's heavy loads were known as 'cuckoos' and today the canal towpath is known as the Cuckoo Way.

It was, however, another engineering genius, George Stephenson, who truly rocketed Chesterfield on to the commercial scene by exploiting the coal and iron ore unearthed whilst digging a tunnel locally for his Leeds to Derby railway line. George spent the last 10 years of his life at Tapton House, which is now part of Chesterfield College, to oversee his 'goldmine'.

From Tapton Lock visitor centre you amble along the Chesterfield Canal for several miles to the Hollingwood Hub, which is an extended lock house that provides a home to the Chesterfield Canal Trust and the popular Nona's coffee shop.

Passing through Ringwood Park, once part of Ringwood Hall – now a hotel – you enter the ancient West Wood. Look out for a pair of striking sculptures of woodland guardians based on Celtic mythology.

Later you cross Tapton Park golf course, where views open up of Derbyshire's largest church complete with its distorted spire that leans at an alarmingly 9 feet and 5 inches from vertical. How it got to be in this precarious-looking position is the subject of many fanciful theories, but let's straighten this story out.

The church was built in the 13th century using unseasoned timber, to which at a later date a backbreaking 32 tonnes of lead tiles were added. Other possible strains on the structure include its lack of cross bracing and a visit by the plague which left less skilled men to complete the work. Nevertheless, the spire still stands tall having weathered coal industry subsidence, two world wars and a fire in 1961!

Just before Chesterfield railway station you'll find a snail you definitely wouldn't want in your garden, as the stainless-steel mollusc spirals some 5½ yards (5m) high. Your final leg of the journey is then back along the Chesterfield Canal towpath.

THE BASICS

Distance: 8 miles / 13km

Gradient: A few minor ascents and descents, but mainly level

Severity: Moderate

Approx. time to walk: 4 hours

Stiles: Two stiles

Maps: OS Landranger 119 (Buxton & Matlock) & 120 (Mansfield & Worksop);
OS Explorer 269 (Chesterfield & Alfreton)

Path description: Good tracks and paths, canal towpath, golf course and lanes.
Much of the route follows the well-signposted Trans Pennine Trail.

Start point: Tapton Lock visitor centre on Lockoford Lane, off A61/A619 (Tesco)
roundabout, Chesterfield (GR SK 387729)

Parking: Courteous roadside parking on Lockoford Lane beside Tapton Lock Visitor
Centre, off A61/A619 (Tesco) roundabout, Chesterfield (S41 7JB)

Dog friendly: Yes, but on lead along road sections and across golf course

Public toilets: Along the Chesterfield Canal towpath – Tapton Lock visitor centre and
at the Hollingwood Hub

Nearest food: Along the Chesterfield Canal towpath – Tapton Lock visitor centre
(light refreshments), The Mill pub at Brimington Wharf and Nona's coffee shop at the
Hollingwood Hub

PUBLIC BRIDLEWAY
Brimington
Shops ¾ mile

PUBLIC BRIDLEWAY
New Whittington
Shops ¾ mile

7 CHESTERFIELD WALK

ROUTE

1. From Tapton Lock visitor centre head north – signed Hollingwood Hub 2.5 miles/ Istanbul 2,500 miles – along the canal towpath passing various locks to reach the Hollingwood Hub at the Hollingwood Lock.

2. Leave the canal here and turn right along the road, which leads to the A619. Cross the road with care into Ringwood Park and proceed past a car park barrier along a surfaced track. By a small parking area veer left off the track along a tree-lined path next to Ringwood Lake. Go left at the end of the lake and at a public footpath sign double-back right. Initially ascend through woodland and then stick ahead across an open area and over a footbridge into West Wood.

3. At a junction maintain direction down steps, cross a footbridge and then bear left up steps. At the next path intersection, near Trough Brook, divert left and continue past several marker posts to an unsigned fork. Here branch left uphill to a large junction with two tall sculptures.  Turn right down the signed Trans Pennine Trail (TPT) and go over Trough Brook to exit the woodland by a large gate onto a road.

4. The well-signed TPT guides you along the route. Turn right along Brooke Drive and follow it as it curves left to a road junction. Jink right and left onto Recreation Road and then take the next left onto Grove Way. Go right at a crossroads to soon join a track.

5. Ignore the first footpath left and take the second (with TPT sign) through a gate. The path swerves right and left to another gate. Turn right and at the end of a fishing pond walk left along a surfaced lane. Watch out for a footpath that crosses the lane. Go left over two stiles and maintain direction at a path intersection to a lane.

6. Walk left and when the lane bends left, bear right onto Tapton Park golf course. Track the TPT signs downhill – Chesterfield's crooked spire comes into view – later passing the practice range and clubhouse to follow the club's driveway to a road.

7. Turn right and continue descending to pass a park on the left with a giant snail shell artwork. Go under a railway bridge and divert immediately right over the Rother and then left to a road. Switch left back over the river and cross over to Holbeck Close – signed Tapton Lock visitor centre.

8. At the end of the road join the Chesterfield Canal – signed Cuckoo Way. Cross the canal at a footbridge and curve left with the canal at a junction. After Tapton Mill Bridge head through the Tapton Tunnel to emerge at Tapton Lock visitor centre.

8 DARLEY ABBEY AND DERBY

EXPLORE THE HISTORIC FABRIC OF A SECTION OF THE DERWENT VALLEY MILLS WORLD HERITAGE SITE (WHS) BETWEEN DARLEY ABBEY MILLS AND THE DERBY SILK MILL. VISIT DERBY'S CATHEDRAL QUARTER AND DELIGHT IN THE BROAD SWEEP OF DARLEY PARK, WHICH BOASTS BRITAIN'S LARGEST COLLECTION OF HYDRANGEAS.

Little remains of the Augustinian Darley Abbey that became the richest and most powerful abbey in Derbyshire, but the settlement was to evolve into an important textile mill complex and custom-made village that is now a much-sought-after satellite of the city of Derby.

Of all the Lower Derwent's pioneering former cotton mills and settlements holding WHS status, the Darley Abbey Mills are the best preserved. Yet despite being entwined in a wonderful setting alongside Darley Park they don't draw the same swell of visitors as Richard Arkwright's Matlock Bath/Cromford empire at the northern gateway to the WHS.

Here in 1782 Thomas Evans set up the Boar's Head cotton mill on the eastern bank of the Derwent. Then, to attract a regular workforce, Evans tempted workers and their families by building desirable residences, including an unheard-of sewage disposal system, on the opposite riverbank. Whilst the Evans' enterprise later passed out of the family's hands, textile production continued until 1970 at the mill complex, which lives on today as a hive of assorted small light businesses.

Thomas lived in a house – now demolished – overlooking the mills and village, but his grandson purchased Darley Hall, which later suffered the same fate. Its parkland beside the Derwent, however, became the public Darley Park, which separates Darley Abbey from Derby's city centre. Tea rooms now occupy land on which the hall was built and in the nearby garden area you'll find over 400 species of hydrangea that form part of the National Hydrangea Collection.

Next door to Derby's cathedral is the Silk Museum. It stands on the site where in 1721 John Lombe threaded the various components of cotton manufacture together to create the world's first factory. Unfortunately, his prototype construction was largely destroyed by fire in 1910 and although the current premises has been home to an exhibition celebrating Derby's industrial heritage, it is at present closed for major redevelopment and due to reopen in 2020. The local community, under professional guidance, has been empowered to 'make' a museum that tells the personal story of their home city.

Your short circuit between Darley Abbey and the city centre's Cathedral Quarter follows the banks of the Derwent providing many different perspectives on this rich heritage landscape.

THE BASICS

Distance: 3½ miles / 5.5km

Gradient: Easy going with a gentle ascent and descent to end the walk

Severity: Easy

Approx. time to walk: 1¾ hours

Stiles: None

Maps: OS Landranger 128 (Derby & Burton upon Trent); OS Explorer 259 (Derby)

Path description: Surfaced and unsurfaced paths close to the River Derwent. Darley Park is prone to seasonal mud.

Start point: Car park just off Darley Street, near the River Derwent at Darley Abbey (GR SK 352383)

Parking: Car park just off Darley Street, near the River Derwent at Darley Abbey (DE22 1DU)

Dog friendly: Yes, but on leads along roads and in Darley Park – as requested by signs – close to the cafe terrace, stables, sports facilities and gardens

Public toilets: To the rear of Darley Park tea room

Nearest food: The Abbey Inn and the Paper Mill pub at Darley Abbey, Darley Park tea room and various just off the route in Derby city centre

8 DARLEY ABBEY AND DERBY WALK

ROUTE

1. Turn right out of the car park onto Darley Street passing The Abbey pub and a viewing area across the Derwent's weir to the Boar's Head mills. Bear right across a footbridge over the river – you are unlikely to be asked to pay the requested toll – to enter the mill complex. Shortly after exiting this business area, turn right onto Folly Road – signed for the city centre. A path veers left and guides you back over the Derwent via the Folly Road footbridge along a surfaced path by the river. At a fork branch right to remain beside the waterway to a T-junction by a large fingerpost.

2. Walk left – signed Darley Abbey. On meeting a road go right for Chester Green. Bear right at a T-junction heading towards Derby Cathedral. Do not go over St Mary's Bridge to your right, but instead cross the road and join the walkway along the left-hand side of Phoenix Street under the A601. Immediately after the underpass again cross the highway to the path opposite and follow it over the Derwent via Cathedral Green Footbridge. In front of the cathedral is a striking statue of Bonnie Prince Charlie (See Walk 19 for details of the Young Pretender's connection to the area). And to your right is the equally imposing Derby Silk Mill.

3. When you are ready to move on, pick up the signed riverside path beside the Silk Mill. Just after Handyside Bridge you pass the Derby Rowing Club to enter Darley Park. After 100 yards head away from the river for 75 yards to a higher-level path and turn right. When this path is no longer visible on the ground, maintain direction across the grass towards the Derby tea rooms. Nearing these premises again veer left to a surfaced path that leads past the tea rooms and the hydrangea gardens to exit the park gates.

4. Cross New Road and walk along Abbey Lane. Just past Old Lane you can visit St Matthew's Church and its war memorial. Return to Old Lane and head down to Darley Street. Turn right back past the Abbey pub to the car park.

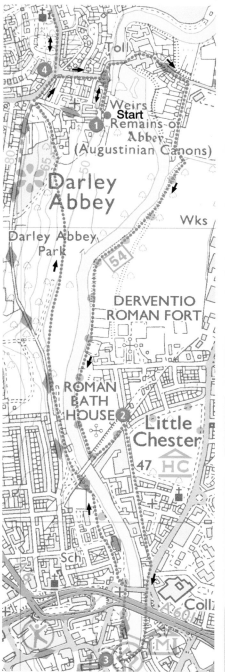

9 ELVASTON CASTLE COUNTRY PARK

Scandalised by his marriage to an actress, the flamboyant Regency Buck 'Beau' Petersham withdrew from high society to live in seclusion with his wife at Elvaston Castle, where he created theatrical pleasure gardens dedicated to the love of his life.

Up until 1939 the Elvaston estate had been the country seat of the Stanhope family – later Earls of Harrington – for 400 years. It was the 3rd Earl who during the 19th century conceived the Gothic revival masterpiece we see today, wrapped around an earlier 17th-century house.

His heir, Viscount Petersham, had earned himself a reputation as a dandy, who gave his trendsetting name to the Petersham coat and Harrington hat. But on becoming the 4th Earl Harrington, he found himself shunned by his social circle when he married the London actress Maria Foote.

Lancelot 'Capability' Brown had turned down a commission by the 3rd Earl to transform the Elvaston estate because he felt the land was too flat. So, with a blank canvas to work with, the now reclusive 4th Earl employed the landscape architect William Barron and a team of ninety gardeners to fashion a fantasy landscape around his Gothic 'castle'.

To the south of the stately home they laid out romantically themed 'garden rooms', including an Italian garden based on designs from Tuscany and an Alhambra garden complete with a Moorish temple. Then in the wider parkland, and with an employer keen to see the set construction scenery quickly erected, Barron established a ground-breaking technique to uproot mature trees, sometimes hundreds of years old, and move them a number of miles to Elvaston. This enabled him to plant several avenues of trees and to stage walks around a lake surrounded by woodland and decorated with rockwork and statues. It must have been quite a 'performance' because when the 5th Earl opened the gardens to the public, visitors flocked despite the pricey three-shilling admission fee.

The Stanhopes left Elvaston for Ireland at the outbreak of the Second World War, during which it became a teacher-training college. Following a period of decline, Derbyshire County Council purchased the estate and established it in 1970 as one of Britain's earliest country parks.

Whilst the house isn't open to the public (except the tea rooms), the mix of formal gardens, woodland and parkland provides plenty of interest alongside an optional circuit of an area set aside as a local nature reserve. Please note dogs are not permitted on the nature reserve. Detailed maps of both the country park and nature reserve are available at www.derbyshire.gov.uk/elvaston. These will provide you with additional information to fully explore all the park's nooks and crannies.

THE BASICS

Distance: 3½ miles / 5.5km (county park and local nature reserve), or 2¼ miles / 3.5km (country park only – dogs are not permitted in the local nature reserve)

Gradient: Level throughout

Severity: Easy

Approx. time to walk: 2 hours for country park and local nature reserve

Stiles: None

Maps: OS Landranger 129 (Nottingham & Loughborough); OS Explorer 259 (Derby)

Path description: Good country park and local nature reserve path network. The local nature reserve is prone to seasonal mud.

Start point: Elvaston Castle Country Park car park, off the B5010 near Elvaston village (GR SK 412331)

Parking: Elvaston Castle Country Park car park, off the B5010 near Elvaston village (DE72 3EN)

Dog friendly: Yes, in the country park, but dogs are not permitted in the local nature reserve

Public toilets: Car park entrance, castle building adjacent to Wyatt's tea rooms, castle courtyard

Nearest food: Wyatt's tea rooms in the castle building

9 ELVASTON CASTLE COUNTRY PARK WALK

ROUTE

1. From the pedestrian crossing by the car park entrance turn left along a track. Stick ahead at a surfaced track around the wooded perimeter of the park's showground.

2. At a large crossroads, you have the option, if you don't have a dog, to complete a loop around the local nature reserve, or go straight ahead (* move to route instruction 4). Go right for the nature reserve and then left through a small gate by its welcome board. A hide on your left grants a view over a heronry and you might also see a kingfisher.

3. Just after crossing a bridge bear right at a T-junction. At a path intersection, which you will later return to, maintain direction. Pass over a bridge and follow a grassy path as it curves left around the boundary of Gretricks Field. At a fork shortly after an information board bend left again to a marker post. Continue forwards, ignoring two right turns at marker posts signed first for the reed beds and then the holly arch to a junction you were at earlier in this route instruction.

4. Branch right to retrace your steps to a junction where you bear left over a bridge to later exit the reserve and turn right back to the crossroads at the start of route instruction 2. Walk right, signed park centre and castle, * or if you haven't completed the nature reserve loop go straight ahead, over a bridge and through a picnic area.

5. At the junction by Springthorpe's Cottage head right and, ignoring all offshoots, follow the surfaced driveway as it curves left past Elvaston cricket ground. The lane then swerves left again at a path intersection to reach the ornate Golden Gates.

6. Pass through the pedestrian access gate next to the main gate. Walk either side of a small grassy area and continue forwards along Vault Avenue towards Elvaston Castle, part of which is visible ahead. Go under Crown Arch into the Parterre Garden with a fine view of the house and the tower of St Bartholomew's Church. Walk up to the front of the mansion (Wyatt's tea rooms) and turn left, then go right into the courtyard. The information centre and shop is under the arch to your left, but your route heads diagonally right to exit the courtyard via one of three adjacent arches.

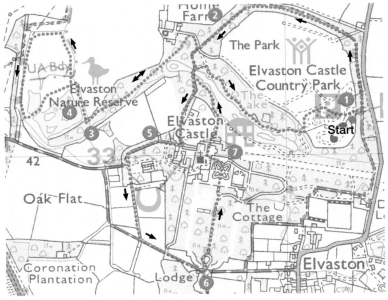

7. Divert left down steps to the lakeside path and turn left. Go through the azalea garden and at the end of the lake negotiate a gate, head right over a bridge and then turn immediate right through another gate to rejoin the lakeside path – signed car park. Approaching the far end of the lake and its boathouse, veer left back into the parking area.

10 EREWASH VALLEY

A LEISURELY LOOP AROUND THE EREWASH VALLEY TO ENJOY THE CONTRASTING CHARACTERS OF TWO CANALS – THE NAVIGABLE EREWASH CANAL, WHICH RUNS ALONG THE URBAN FRINGE OF ILKESTON, AND THE TRANQUIL LOCAL NATURE RESERVE OF THE ABANDONED NOTTINGHAM CANAL.

The meandering River Erewash marks the border with Derbyshire to its west and Nottinghamshire to the east. It's a valley with a rich industrial heritage, which initially harnessed the river to power various mills, but when local coal became king it also provided an ideal transport corridor for canals to access the Trent and later, of course, the railways.

Straddling the river, nowadays the valley's canals carry much lighter loads along the 30-mile circular and traffic-free Erewash Valley Trail. This walk takes advantage of the close proximity of these canals to create a mainly towpath-based route with connecting shortcuts across the river.

Your start point is the Nottingham Canal on the Nottinghamshire side of the Erewash, but you immediately leave this waterway to cross the river into Derbyshire to meet the Erewash Canal. Between the two canals the scene is dominated by the Bennerley Viaduct that spans the valley between Cotmanhay and Awsworth.

Built in 1877, this giant structure is one of only two remaining wrought-iron viaducts in England. It has been disused since 1968, but recently the sustainable transport Sustrans unveiled plans to give this iconic monument a new lease of life as part of the national cycle network. Unfortunately a bid to the Heritage Lottery Fund was unsuccessful, but The Friends of Bennerley Viaduct are still hoping to find a future use for the landmark structure.

To the north of the viaduct is Langley Mill, where the northern end of both the Erewash and Nottingham canals join Derbyshire's Cromford Canal at the Great Northern Basin. Heading south along the roughly 12-mile-long Erewash Canal, which links into the River Trent at Trent Lock, you follow its surfaced towpath along the edge of the hilltop town of Ilkeston passing the odd barge, swans aplenty and maybe even a kingfisher.

Leaving the canal at the Gallows Inn, believed to be a location where a gallows once stood, you soon reach the Nottingham Canal. This was designed as a contour canal and as such it hugs the side of the valley, which reduced the need to construct locks and handily provides an elevated view over Ilkeston and the surrounding countryside. Six miles of this 15-mile-long disused canal that runs from Langley Mill to the city of Nottingham is a designated local nature reserve. Your return leg through this untamed wildlife corridor is a delight to follow and offers a quieter canalside perspective than the busier scene on the Erewash.

THE BASICS

Distance: 5½ miles / 9km

Gradient: Virtually level throughout

Severity: Easy to moderate based on distance

Approx. time to walk: 2¾ hours

Stiles: None

Maps: OS Landranger 129 (Nottingham & Loughborough); OS Explorer 260 (Nottingham)

Path description: Good towpaths, one of which is surfaced, and road walking. Newtons Lane at the start of the walk is intermittently pavemented and can get busy.

Start point: Nottingham Canal local nature reserve car park on Newtons Lane, just off the A6096 (signed Cotmanhay) between Ilkeston and Awsworth (GR SK 476433)

Parking: Nottingham Canal local nature reserve car park on Newtons Lane, just off the A6096 (signed Cotmanhay) between Ilkeston and Awsworth (near NG16 2SB)

Dog friendly: Yes, but on leads for road sections

Public toilets: Gallows Inn playing fields, Nottingham Road (A609), Ilkeston

Nearest food: Gallows Inn, Nottingham Road (A609), Ilkeston – adjacent to Erewash Canal

10 EREWASH VALLEY WALK

ROUTE

1. Exit the car park onto Newtons Lane. An optional there-and-back extension along the canal towpath opposite visits a viewing area for the Bennerley Viaduct. Otherwise, turn left along the lane to cross the Erewash and a railway bridge – taking care where there is no pavement – into the industrial outskirts of Ilkeston. After passing Ilkeston Town FC go left at a humpback bridge onto the Erewash Canal towpath.

2. Follow the surfaced path beside the waterway for several miles along the outskirts of Ilkeston to reach the Gallows Inn on the A609. Turn left to pass the Gallows Inn playing fields and when the road curves right just after the Erewash, keep ahead onto a signed footpath over a railway bridge. Cross a track and gently climb up to the Nottingham Canal.

3. Turn left along the towpath to pass a few small ponds and then two small car parks. Later the waterway follows a U-bend near the village of Cossall and then runs alongside woodland. Go over a road bridge to the A6096 and use the pedestrian crossing to rejoin the canal opposite. With the Bennerley Viaduct soon coming into view, turn right at Newtons Lane back to your start point.

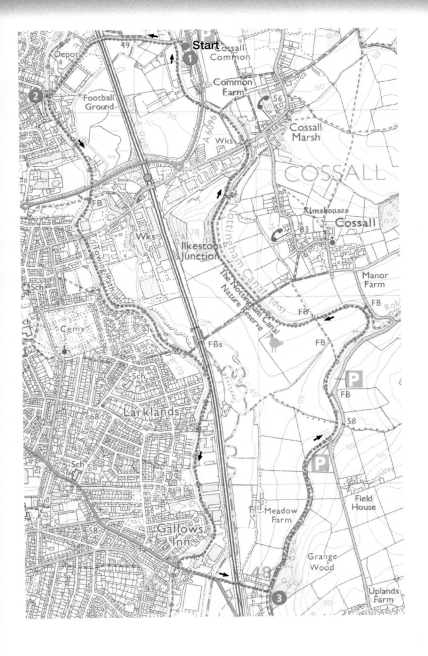

11 FIVE PITS TRAIL

FROM RAIL TO TRAIL, THE FIVE PITS GREENWAY ROUGHLY TRACKS THE LINE OF THE GREAT CENTRAL RAILWAY, WHICH SERVED FIVE DEEP COLLIERIES – GRASSMOOR, WILLIAMTHORPE, HOLMEWOOD, PILSLEY AND TIBSHELF – IN A FORMER HEARTLAND OF 'BLACK GOLD'.

Shaped like a lollipop, this 7½-mile (12.1km) trail begins at Tibshelf and heads north to circle around Wolfie Pond (with an offshoot to Grassmoor Country Park), Williamthorpe local nature reserve and Holmewood Woodlands.

It's a pleasant route in its own right, but such was the extent of the north-east Derbyshire/ Nottinghamshire coalfields that the Five Pits Trail (FPT) directly links into the Silverhill and Pleasley–Teversal Trails. Collectively, this extensive web of off-road multi-user trails, covering in excess of 20 miles, is known as the Phoenix Greenways and represents the 'green' vigour with which the phoenix has risen from the ashes.

Your route begins at Grassmoor Country Park at the northern end of the FPT and gently rolls, on account of its earlier land use, around the 'boiled sweet' at the end of the 'lollipop stick' to visit three of the trail's five pit sites – Grassmoor, Williamthorpe and Holmewood.

An initial short loop explores the country park's two ponds, grassland and woodland habitats before joining the FPT. After passing the Wolfie fishing lake you enter Williamthorpe's local nature reserve where a mosaic of ponds, reed beds and woodland await. At Holmewood Woodlands what you see isn't the original Holme Wood, as this was felled to make way for the coal mine, but is a maturing fresh start.

THE BASICS

Distance: 6½ miles / 10.5km

Gradient: Gently undulating with benches aplenty

Severity: Moderate

Approx. time to walk: 3¼ hours

Stiles: None

Maps: OS Landranger 120 (Mansfield & Worksop); OS Explorer 269 (Chesterfield & Alfreton)

Path description: Excellent multi-user trail with a number of road crossings

Start point: Car park at Grassmoor Country Park, off Birkin Lane between Temple Normanton and Grassmoor village (GR SK 412672)

Parking: Car park at Grassmoor Country Park, off Birkin Lane between Temple Normanton and Grassmoor village (S42 5DA)

Dog friendly: Yes, but on leads near roads and through the Williamthorpe local nature reserve

Public toilets: None

Nearest food: None en route, but try the Shoulder pub at Hardstoft near Tibshelf or the Hardwick Inn on the edge of the Hardwick Hall estate

ROUTE

1. Facing a small pond at the end of the car park, walk half-left along a grassy path past a picnic bench to a footbridge. Cross the bridge and turn left to walk next to a larger pond. Continue past a bench beyond the pond to shortly reach a main track and double-back left. Go right on meeting a marker post and stick ahead to a main junction (marker post) on the edge of the country park. Bear left and follow this track as it curves left to a road bridge on your right.

2. Go under the bridge and follow the Five Pits Trail (FPT) as it gradually rises to a large triangular junction by a small parking area. Branch left and left again in a few yards, with Wolfie angling pond on your right. Pass under a road to a T-junction and veer right into Williamthorpe nature reserve.

3. Look out for a bench from which there is a viewpoint over another fishing pond. When the path begins to descend, ignore a left turn and cross a footbridge. Turn immediate right beside the fishing pond and then a nature reserve lake. At a junction just after the lake divert left.

4. Head right at a crossroads – signed FPT Holmewood – and bend left at a cautionary sign for a forthcoming road. Go right along the pavement over a road bridge and immediately cross over to rejoin the FPT. Shortly cross another road and again link back up with the FPT into Holmewood Woodlands. At an FPT Tibshelf sign maintain direction alongside a playing field.

5. Cross over a road – Crich Stand can be seen in the distance – and return to the FPT. Fork right and right again at a triangular junction – FPT Grassmoor – and maintain direction at the next junction by a picnic bench. The trail now winds its way to the final road crossing where once again you pick up the FPT opposite.

6. At the junction you were at earlier by Wolfie Pond jink left and then right and descend the trail to retrace your steps back under the bridge into Grassmoor Country Park. Turn right to return to the car park.

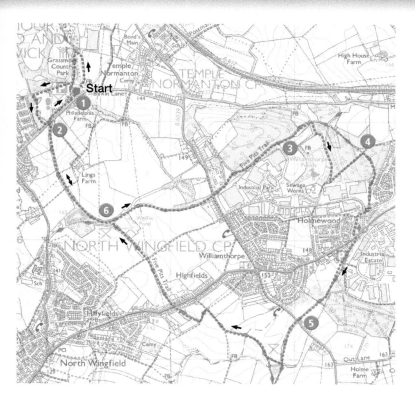

12 LINACRE RESERVOIRS

SECLUDED IN A SHELTERED VALLEY, THE LINACRE TRIO OF
RESERVOIRS, SURROUNDED BY ATTRACTIVE WOODLAND, ARE
IDEAL FOR A STROLL AT ANY TIME OF THE YEAR, BUT THE
OPPORTUNITY TO IMMERSE YOURSELF IN THE SPRINGTIME
OCEAN OF BLUEBELLS OR AUTUMN RIOT OF COLOUR IS NOT TO
BE MISSED.

Linacre means arable land where flax was grown, and as early as the 13th century linen, made from the stalk of the flax plant, was being produced in the valley. During medieval times Linacre Hall stood on what is now the Middle Linacre Woods car park. Later this property was superseded by Linacre House, which was the birthplace of Dr Thomas Linacre, who led a distinguished career as a physician to some prominent personalities of the day, including Henry VIII, and went on to establish the Royal College of Physicians.

Linacre's valley remained a rural backwater until the mid-19th century when Chesterfield's industrial and population growth began to accelerate and demands to increase its water supply rose accordingly. Fortunately, the solution was on the doorstep as the Linacre Valley, fed by water that runs off nearby moorland, provided a suitable catchment area.

The reservoirs – Upper, Middle and Lower – were built one at a time between 1855 and 1904. Then in 1909, after grumbles about the taste and odour of the water – it was said that poor people used the water for soup, the middle classes bathed in it and the rich folk watered their gardens with it – a sand and chlorination filtration plant was installed.

Yet by 1995 Chesterfield's thirsty residents had swelled to a level which couldn't be satisfied by Linacre's chain of reservoirs and the town's H_2O is now supplied from elsewhere. Severn Trent Water continue to maintain the site as a safe haven for nature and a recreational amenity.

Your straightforward outing wriggles its leisurely way around these small but perfectly formed bodies of water, mainly through woodland, with views opening up of each individual reservoir around its dam wall. The valley, however, is crisscrossed by numerous footpaths providing options aplenty to roam the wider locality. One pleasant alternative is to extend your walk in the direction of Chesterfield to the reclaimed opencast mining site at Holmebrook Valley Park.

THE BASICS

Distance: 2¾ miles / 4.5km

Severity: Easy

Approx. time to walk: 1½ hours

Stiles: None

Maps: OS Landranger 119 (Buxton & Matlock); OS Explorer 269 (Chesterfield & Alfreton) or OL24 The Peak District (White Peak Area)

Path description: Good network of woodland paths and boardwalks cared for by Severn Trent Water

Start point: Middle or Lower Linacre Woods car parks (top car park allocated to season ticket holders), off the B6050 near Cutthorpe (GR SK 335728)

Parking: Middle or Lower Linacre Woods car parks (top car park allocated to season ticket holders), off the B6050 near Cutthorpe (S42 7JW)

Dog friendly: Yes, but on leads around the upper reservoir, which is managed as a nature reserve

Public toilets: Ranger's office by the Lower Linacre Woods car park near the end of the walk

Nearest food: None en route, but pubs nearby at Cutthorpe and a pub and very popular cafe at Barlow (booking recommended)

ROUTE

1. Exit the Middle car park via a gate just beyond a Linacre Reservoirs information board and descend the lane, with an outlook across Chesterfield, to the bottom car park. Next to another information board join a stepped path into woodland. At a T-junction with a wide track, go right to reach the dam wall of the Middle reservoir.

2. Keep ahead and as you approach the wall of the top reservoir swing right by steps. In a few yards at a path intersection turn left to walk above the reservoir shoreline. Drop down to an inlet, cross the lower of two footbridges, and proceed to the end of this body of water. Cross the footbridge on your left over Birley Brook and follow the concessionary path/boardwalk as it hugs the edge of the Upper reservoir back to its dam wall.

3. Continue on the clear footpath through trees to the dam wall of the Middle reservoir. Maintain direction, briefly dipping down and then back up, to a junction. Ignoring the steps to your right, look out for the frequent yellow waymarkers painted on the tree trunks, which are a helpful guide if the woods are carpeted with leaf litter, close to the Lower reservoir. At a fork, branch left to its dam wall and cross the embankment. Climb the steps at the far side of the reservoir – the Ranger's Office and toilet facilities are to the right – but you veer left and ascend a lane that leads back to the Lower and Middle car parks.

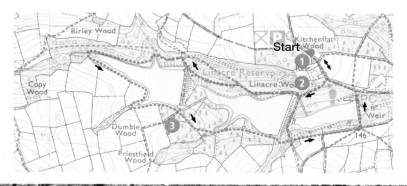

13 MELBOURNE

IT MAY NOT HAVE THE SUNSHINE RECORD OF THE AUSSIE CITY TO WHICH IT GAVE ITS MONIKER – CHOSEN BY QUEEN VICTORIA IN HONOUR OF HER PRIME MINISTER LORD MELBOURNE – BUT THE GEORGIAN TOWN OF MELBOURNE OFFERS AMPLE OPPORTUNITIES TO RELAX AND ENJOY YOURSELF.

Standing in the town's Church Square is arguably one of England's finest Norman parish churches. Neighbouring this is Melbourne Hall, which was developed during the 18th century on the site of a bishop's palace by the Coke family. Nowadays this country house is the home of Lord and Lady Ralph Kerr, who are direct descendants of the Coke dynasty.

Lord Melbourne – William Lamb – became Queen Victoria's first prime minister when she succeeded to the throne in 1837 at the tender age of 18. It's often said that William was her favourite head of government as he took on the role of mentoring the politically inexperienced young monarch, although he was well known for ladling flattery on the queen to influence her decision-making. Melbourne's wife – Lady Caroline Lamb – also achieved notoriety in her day for a scandalous public affair with the flamboyant poet Lord Byron.

Through marriage, Melbourne Hall later passed to Lord Palmerston, who coincidently also became prime minister during Queen Victoria's reign, although her relationship with him was perhaps not so cordial as she once referred to him as 'that dreadful old man'.

Before heading off on the main route, a short detour to the rear of Melbourne Hall provides a viewpoint over the mansion and its magnificent gardens complete with an unusual wrought-iron 'birdcage' arbour. (The gardens are open to the public during the summer and the hall may be visited during August.)

Returning to Church Square you pass in-between the hall, which is hidden from sight, and the landscaped former mill pond – The Pool. Field paths lead you to the hamlet of Wilson, but along this stretch the isolated outcrop of Breedon on the Hill can be seen just over the Leicestershire border. Over time this rock formation has been the site of an Iron Age fort, a monastery and a priory, but it is now crowned by its parish church.

After Wilson you join the 13-mile Derby to Worthington Cloud Trail, which follows the disused Derby to Ashby branch railway. Departing the trail at Melbourne you climb up through the town's narrow streets to the market cross close to your start point.

Another of Melbourne's Victorian claims to fame is that it was birthplace of Thomas Cook, the 'Father of Modern Tourism'. Melbourne, therefore, truly is a town with international connections, where aeroplanes fly low as they head in and out of the East Midlands airport.

THE BASICS

Distance: 6 miles / 10km

Gradient: Mainly level with one moderate ascent

Severity: Moderate

Approx. time to walk: 3 hours

Stiles: Seven

Maps: OS Landranger 128 (Derby & Burton upon Trent) & 129 (Nottingham & Loughborough); OS Explorer 245 (National Forest)

Path description: Well-signed field paths and tracks, a multi-user surfaced trail and lanes

Start point: Church Square, off the junction of Church Street, Castle Street and Blackwell Lane, Melbourne (GR SK 389250)

Parking: Church Square, off the junction of Church Street, Castle Street and Blackwell Lane, Melbourne (DE73 8JH), or other public parking in Melbourne

Dog friendly: Yes, if they can manage a number of good field stiles, but on leads if livestock is present and along lanes

Public toilets: None

Nearest food: Melbourne Hall tea rooms, the Bulls Head pub at Wilson and pubs and cafes in Melbourne

ROUTE

1. If you wish to view Melbourne Hall and its gardens, turn right out of Church Square onto Blackwell Lane. In 200 yards go right at a footpath sign and in 75 yards a wonderful outlook of the country house opens up. Retrace your steps to Church Square and follow the signpost to The Pool past the church to soon reach the former mill pond. Ignore the path at the end of the pond, and shortly after branch right through a gate into a field.

2. Cross two fields via stiles and in the third field follow the path towards the field boundary adjacent to woodland. Just before a field corner look out for a stile on your left. After the stile the path jinks right then left and you then maintain direction along a tree-lined

track into a field. Close to the end of this field, fork right to a stile in 10 yards. Walking next to woodland, climb a stile to reach the far corner of the trees.

3. Bear half-left towards a redundant stile and pass through a gap next to it. At a marker post in 10 yards, go left and in a few yards bear right in between gateposts. Climb half-left up a field to a stile and finally head across the middle of the final field to cross a stile out onto a lane.

4. Turn left and when the lane bends right, veer left onto a signed bridleway with a vista across to Breedon on the Hill. In 30 yards turn right at a marker post and then left at the next marker to join an enclosed track, which leads to a golf course. Maintain direction by a hedge and in 100 yards pass through an opening to leave the golf course and walk along the right-hand perimeter of fields. When you are almost level with a farm, the track kinks left and you shortly bear right along a surfaced lane into Wilson.

5. Go left through the hamlet, passing the Bulls Head, and curve left – signed Melbourne – at a junction. In 50 yards, opposite a lay-by, turn right for the Cloud Trail. Divert left onto this surfaced trail and, as you approach a bridge in roughly a mile, fork left to a road on the outskirts of Melbourne.

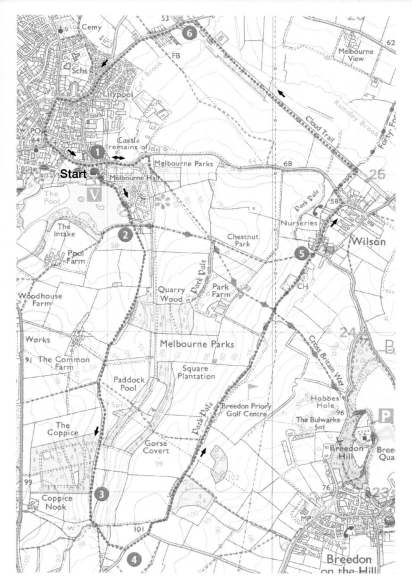

6. Walk left along the road and keep ahead at a junction (Castle Street) surrounding a grassy triangle. At the next junction swing left, signed Ticknall. At the top of Chapel Street go left to the Market Place and turn left again down Church Street back to Church Square.

14 MOSS VALLEY

PUT A SPRING IN YOUR STEP THROUGH THE MOSS VALLEY,
WHERE NATURE ROLLS OUT HER ANNUAL VIBRANT CARPET OF
BLUEBELLS UNDER A SHADY CANOPY OF ANCIENT WOODLAND.
IT'S A NATIONAL FAVOURITE THAT FILLS THE AIR WITH A SWEET
PERFUME AND THIS IS ONE OF THE COUNTY'S TOP SPOTS TO
EXPERIENCE BLUEBELL HEAVEN.

The Moss Brook meanders east for five miles from the southern outskirts of Sheffield to
enter the River Rother near Eckington. It's a rural wildlife corridor supporting woodland,
including the Moss Valley Woodlands nature reserve, and agriculture.

Your route begins roughly in the centre of the valley at the hamlet of Ford and explores
the highs and lows of the eastern end of the valley. The name Moss Brook, meaning a
stream through marshy land, offers a clue as to the wet ground conditions that may be
encountered during the winter.

Laced with paths and tracks worn by
generations of workers, at one time the
valley's watercourse powered eight mills
specialising in the grinding of scythes and
sickles. The local iron industry was so
prolific it's claimed that by 1800 Eckington
produced more nails than anywhere else in
the world. A short optional detour visits the
town's church dedicated to St Peter and St
Paul, which is one of Derbyshire's oldest
buildings.

There's also evidence in the valley on your
return leg beside the Moss Brook of mining
and quarrying. Another quick optional
diversion guides you to the Seldom Seen
engine house of the former Eckington Plumbley Colliery. It's a strangely named relic of the
past, but concealed in woodland it can be a spooky-looking surprise if you aren't expecting
to see it. After this eerie encounter you then pass the spine-chilling Never Fear Dam before
returning to the tranquil pond and picnic area at Ford.

If you have timed your walk to coincide with the sea of bluebells, half a mile from Eckington
church at Renishaw Hall, you'll be even more enchanted by their dazzling display of blue
amid the wider grandeur of the hall's gardens and parkland.

THE BASICS

Distance: 4 miles / 6.5km

Gradient: Gently undulating throughout, but nothing demanding

Severity: Moderate

Approx. time to walk: 2 hours

Stiles: Two

Maps: OS Landranger 111 (Sheffield & Doncaster) & 120 (Mansfield & Worksop); OS Explorer 278 (Sheffield & Barnsley) and the route clips the edge of OS Explorer 269 (Chesterfield & Alfreton), but this is not essential for route finding

Path description: Field and woodland paths – prone to seasonal mud – and lanes

Start point: Car park next to Ford fishing pond, approached from a lane – unsigned – in front of the Bridge Inn on Ridgeway Moor at the hamlet of Ford (GR SK 402803)

Parking: Car park next to Ford fishing pond, approached from a lane – unsigned – in front of the Bridge Inn on Ridgeway Moor at the hamlet of Ford (near S12 3XY)

Dog friendly: Yes, but on leads along road sections

Public toilets: None

Nearest food: Bridge Inn at Ford and the Alma pub at Mosborough

14 MOSS VALLEY WALK

ROUTE

1. Cross the picnic area and walk to the Bridge Inn's car park entrance. Turn right uphill and 20 yards before Sloade Lane on your left, go right onto a signed bridleway. Follow the track, with extensive views east and west along the Moss Valley, to a path intersection. Here the track bends right to another main junction in several hundred yards. Remain ahead on the main track – the first track to your left is on private property – and ascend to a farm at Plumbley.

2. Go through an A-frame at the side of a gate and at a crossroads of paths at the far end of the farm buildings divert right. Descend a track, which eventually leads to housing and a road at Mosborough. Continue along Plumbley Lane, past Marsh Close, to a T-junction and walk right.

3. Turn right at the large village green along Chapel Street, later walking with a grassy bank topped by a white fence on your left. Pass the Alma pub, which affords fine views from its garden over the Moss Valley, and leaving Mosborough's housing behind begin to descend Gas House Lane.

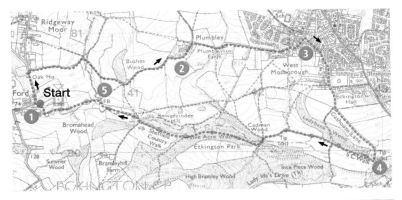

4. At the bottom of the hill the lane bends right and just before reaching the Moss Brook your route is to the right by a barrier, but it's worth a detour 150 yards further along the lane to the Church of St Peter and St Paul at Eckington. Otherwise, head right through woodland above the Moss Brook. Maintain direction at a T-junction and again continue forwards at a fallen tree trunk – marked Sheffield Country Walk. At a marker post, your route once again is straight ahead, but by crossing the footbridge to your left and veering left for 50 yards you can visit the Seldom Seen engine house of the former Eckington Plumbley Colliery.

5. Remain on the main track, which moves uphill away from the river to a junction. Climb a stile on the left and follow the path that quickly rejoins the riverbank across a meadow. Climb a stile and descend through woodland. Disregarding a white footbridge, you soon pass the Never Fear Dam and return to the Ford pond and car park.

15 PLEASLEY VALE

WEAVE YOUR WAY THROUGH A HIDDEN AND LITTLE-KNOWN NATURAL MAGNESIAN LIMESTONE GORGE TO DISCOVER A FORMER TEXTILE MILL COMPLEX AND ITS ASSOCIATED ESTATE VILLAGE – THE BIRTHPLACE OF THE INTERNATIONALLY RECOGNISED FABRIC KNOWN AS VIYELLA.

Soft to the touch and durable, Viyella was registered in 1894 as a blend of 55% merino wool and 45% cotton, making it the world's first branded cloth. The Viyella story began in 1784 when a consortium of businessmen, fronted by Henry Hollins, built a water-powered cotton mill at Pleasley Vale. A second mill followed, but both suffered devastating fires. Henry's grandson, William, capitalised on this misfortune by rebuilding two steam-powered mills and concentrating production on high-end products.

But it was in 1890 that William's nephew, another Henry, took the Hollins and Company business to a whole new level when he built a mill on the unusually named Via Gellia (A5012) road near the Derbyshire town of Matlock. It was 'Via Gellia' which inspired the name 'Viyella', which went on in the 1960s to be awarded the prestigious Royal Warrant.

From Pleasley's village centre and the site of its former corn mill, you initially follow the River Meden before linking into a disused railway line – the Meden Trail – along the southern ridge of Pleasley Vale.

After the trail you clip a corner of Pleasley Vale's estate village where there is a delightful row of cottages and St Chad's Church. Most of the workforce for the mills would have come from nearby Pleasley as, based on the standard of the homes, Pleasley Vale would almost certainly have been reserved for senior employees.

You return to the remains of the village after circling around an isolated section of the vale known as Little Matlock where the exposed cliffs of the limestone gorge, carved out by melting glacial ice caps, can clearly be seen.

Passing a flower-decked war memorial and another terrace of cottages, the valley suddenly becomes deeper and narrower. Visually this provides a natural separation between the estate village and the mill complex. It also dramatically enhances the scale and setting of the three mills and their ponds. Leaving the former industry behind, the valley widens out again and you track the River Meden back to Pleasley.

If you have time, the reclaimed site of the Pleasley Colliery in Pleasley village makes an interesting visit. Its restored headstocks and engine house dominate the landscape for miles around and you can wander around the Pleasley Pit country park, which is designated as a local nature reserve.

THE BASICS

Distance: 4½ miles / 7.2km

Gradient: Mainly flat with a few minor undulations

Severity: Easy

Approx. time to walk: 2½ hours

Stiles: Three

Maps: OS Landranger 120 (Mansfield & Worksop); OS Explorer 270 (Sherwood Forest)

Path description: Multi-user trail, woodland and field paths and quiet lanes. Pleasley Vale mill complex is now a light business park, but is very peaceful at weekends.

Start point: Meden Square (village green), Pleasley village off the A617 (GR SK 505642)

Parking: Courteous roadside parking on Meden Square (village green), Pleasley village off the A617 (NG19 7SR)

Dog friendly: Yes, but on leads along lanes

Public toilets: None

Nearest food: None en route, but pub in Pleasley village

15 PLEASLEY VALE WALK

ROUTE

1. Facing the former Meden Mill and its dam next to Meden Square, cross the road to join the footpath next to the River Meden. Go left at a T-junction, pass through an A-frame and track the watercourse as it curves right. At a marker post veer right away from the river to ascend next to a wall and turn right onto the Meden Trail, which runs along the top of Pleasley Vale to a lane.

2. Walk left down the lane to reach a commemorative stone – 'Pleasley Vale Village 1854' – and a view of the Top Row of the former estate village's cottages. Fork right at a junction to St Chad's Church and join a footpath over a stile into Little Matlock. Follow the Meden to a track and turn left over the river.

3. When the track curves right, go left over a stile into a field and follow the opposite bank of the river to another stile. Now remain close to the exposed limestone cliff and when the faint path appears to veer right, bear left towards a gate in 40 yards in-between the river and a house to a lane.

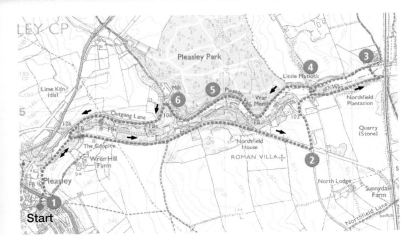

4. Cross over to a footpath (to avoid possible summertime brambles, you can go left along the lane past St Chad's Church and then right at the junction) and bear immediate right to soon walk across a field to a lane.

5. Turn right and walk through the estate village, passing a war memorial and a terrace of cottages, to enter the Pleasley Vale mill complex of three mills (numbered 3, 2 and 1 respectively). The latter two mills retained their ponds. After the final mill – Mill 1 – if you look up to the clifftop to your right there is a large modern house. This is the site of the one-time Vale House, where the mill owner lived and kept a lofty eye over his workers.

6. Leave the mill complex by two lodges and shortly after join a footpath on the left above the Meden (or to avoid possible summertime brambles, continue along Outgang Lane to the car park). Cross a track to reach a car park. Go through the parking area to join a path that soon descends to a bridge over the river and head right to retrace your steps back to Pleasley village by negotiating an A-frame and then turning right into Meden Square.

Delve into a legacy to Old King Coal at Poulter Country Park, with a tip-top viewpoint, undulating meadows renowned for their carpet of springtime cowslips, and wildlife ponds studded with artworks.

Running through the country park is the Archaeological Way, an 11 mile/18.5km multi-user trail between Pleasley Pit country park and Creswell Crags. Along the Way you unearth a wealth of natural and cultural heritage assets from the hunting grounds of Ice Age visitors at the internationally significant Creswell Crags to the rise and fall of the local coalfields.

It's currently a work in progress that will realign a route created in the 1990s – shown on the OS map – to reconnect communities through a greenway corridor. In turn, this will then link into the already extensive Derbyshire/Nottinghamshire off-road trail network.

Poulter's park was landscaped in 1988 on the former Langwith Colliery that extracted coal from 1876 to 1978, and at its height employed 1,300 men. The limestone gorge at Creswell Crags, honeycombed with caves, provides the UK's only known example of cave paintings and this creative theme has also been captured at Poulter where sculptures inspired by the community's landscape, wildlife and history add interest to the parkland.

From the southern end of the country park you pass a stone commemorating the site of a First World War munitions factory that witnessed two tragic explosions resulting in the loss of six lives. It also remembers a nearby Second World War plane crash, which killed its crew.

After a sculpture of a flower based on a locally discovered flint tool you follow the Archaeological Way through the country park to Mag Lane on Whaley Moor. Your route guides you through the small village of Whaley to the River Poulter and the mill pond that powered the former Whaley Mill.

This whole area was once densely wooded and the one-time medieval deer park at Scarcliffe Park is a remaining example. Although the enclosure contains evidence of Bronze Age and Romano-British activity you must stick to the bridleway as the woodland is owned and managed by the Chatsworth estate as a game reserve.

For the final leg of your journey you re-enter Poulter Country Park and climb up to a viewpoint with its Top of the World sculpture dedicated to the early Stone Age. From there it's a downhill run past the unfurling black fern-fronds of Industrial Fossils symbolising coal, a Scimitar Flower representing the park's wildflower meadows and a dragonfly hovering over a pond.

THE BASICS

Distance: 4¼ miles / 6.8km

Gradient: Undulating through Poulter Country Park, otherwise easy going

Severity: Easy to moderate

Approx. time to walk: 2¼ hours

Stiles: None

Maps: OS Landranger 120 (Mansfield & Worksop); OS Explorer 270 (Sherwood Forest)

Path description: Poulter Country Park path network, woodland and quiet lanes

Start point: Poulter Country Park car park, Whaley Road, off the A632 at Langwith (GR SK 524704)

Parking: Poulter Country Park car park, Whaley Road, off the A632 at Langwith (NG20 9HS)

Dog friendly: Yes, but on leads along lanes, near the railway line and through Scarcliffe Park, which is managed for game

Public toilets: None

Nearest food: None en route, but the idyllically located Jug & Glass inn at Nether Langwith is recommended

ROUTE

1. From the car park, and standing with your back to the Poulter Country Park/ Archaeological Way information board, turn right to gently ascend a main path that winds past a commemorative stone and then a flower sculpture near the brow of the hill. The path then begins to descend and you keep ahead at a junction by a bench to reach the Langwith–Whaley Thorns Railway station. Disregard the bridge and go left – signed Archaeological Way – beside the railway line. Later the trail bends left away from the railway, descends and then swings right back to the train line to meet Mag Lane.

2. Turn left along the lane to a road junction and bear left – signed Whaley. Nearing the village disregard the first lane to your left, and take the next left in the village centre – signed Nether Langwith.

3. Opposite Park House turn right onto the signed bridleway. At the entrance to Red Brick Cottage turn left to walk above the Poulter and an old mill pond. Close to

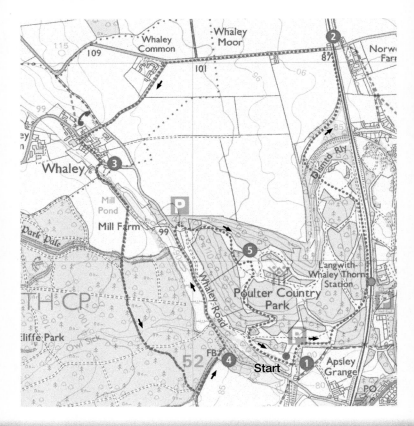

the end of the lake, bear right across a field towards the trees of Scarcliffe Park. Follow the bridleway through the woodland, maintaining direction at two marker posts. At the far side of the wood turn left and follow its edge down to Whaley Road.

4. Turn left and just before Mill Farm turn right into a car park for Poulter Country Park. Cross the car park to a gate and branch left uphill. Keep ahead when a converging track comes in from the right. At a marker post fork right and at the next marker post go left to the Top of the World sculpture.

5. Based on your direction of approach to the sculpture, to your right you can see two marker posts 30 yards away. Head downhill towards the right-hand post and continue to another marker in 25 yards near the Industrial Fossils artwork. Continue descending and follow the path as it bends right and passes a 'Sculpture Trail' sign. Keep ahead at the Scimitar Flower to a series of wildlife ponds – and dragonfly sculpture – back to your start point.

17 SHARDLOW

Immerse yourself in 18th-century heritage at Shardlow, once the bustling inland terminal port of the Trent and Mersey Canal, where today its colourful waterfront proudly showcases some of Britain's best-preserved canal architecture.

Britain's first modern canal – the Bridgewater Canal – which ran from the Duke of Bridgewater's Worsley coalmines to Manchester was engineered by James Brindley. Seeing the potential of this pioneering trade route, Brindley, Derbyshire born near Buxton, masterminded an inland link between the east and west ports of Hull and Liverpool by connecting the Trent, which flows into the Humber Estuary, to the Mersey.

Although Brindley didn't live to see his 93½-mile-long vision come to fruition in 1777, he had many backers for his ambitious artificial waterway, including the likes of Josiah Wedgwood, who was keen to see its route service his pottery empire in Stoke-on-Trent.

Shardlow sits close to the Derwent Mouth – the confluence of the Trent and Derwent – and the junction of the River Trent and the Trent and Mersey canal, which made it an ideal transhipment point between broad river boats and narrow canal boats. To facilitate this changeover, warehousing for temporary storage was built at Shardlow and over time merchants' houses, workers' cottages and many inns were added to this bustling community.

Inevitably, with the coming of the railways the canal's trade began to decline in the 1840s, and when the North Staffordshire Railway Company purchased the canal in 1847 that signalled the end of the waterway's commercial life.

Quickly joining the canal – the picturesque and brightly coloured former port area is saved for the walk's finale – you head out of the village to the Derwent Mouth. The Derwent, a major tributary of the Trent, is Derbyshire's longest river and home to the Derwent Valley Mills World Heritage Site (see walks 3 and 8), Chatsworth House and the Upper Derwent Dams, to name just a few of its star attractions. Crossing the Trent via Long Horse Bridge, you follow the river upstream to the heart of Shardlow.

What makes Shardlow unique is that most of its port and associated buildings survive. Fittingly, Shardlow Heritage Centre occupies the oldest canal building in the village – the salt warehouse. Opposite this is the former Clock Warehouse, now a waterfront pub and an ideal spot to enjoy post-walk refreshments.

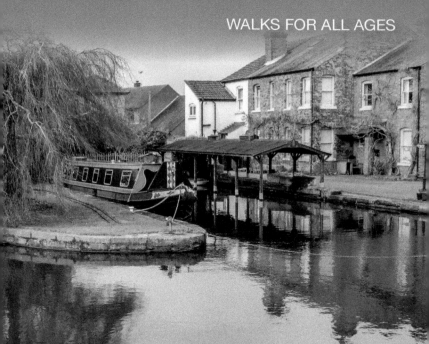

THE BASICS

Distance: 2½ miles / 4km

Gradient: Level throughout

Severity: Easy

Approx. time to walk: 1¼ hours

Stiles: One

Maps: OS Landranger 129 (Nottingham & Loughborough); OS Explorer 260 (Nottingham). A small section of the walk is detailed on OS Explorer 245 (The National Forest), but this map is not required if you carefully follow the route instructions.

Path description: Canal towpath, riverbank and road

Start point: Wilne Lane car park, off the B5010 by the Navigation Inn at Shardlow (GR SK 445304)

Parking: Wilne Lane car park, off the B5010 by the Navigation Inn at Shardlow (near DE72 2HH)

Dog friendly: Yes, but on leads along road section

Public toilets: None

Nearest food: Several pubs passed en route in Shardlow, plus there are other refreshment opportunities in the village

17 SHARDLOW WALK

ROUTE

1. Head right out of the car park along Wilne Lane. Just before a bridge, bear left down steps onto the Trent and Mersey Canal. Walk right along the towpath passing Chapel Farm marina, bridge 1 and the Derwent Mouth Lock to reach the Derwent Mouth.

2. Here the path curves right towards Long Horse Bridge. Cross the bridge over the Trent and at a T-junction turn right to walk along a track beside the river. At a marker post branch right to remain by the Trent and go through a small gate at the next marker post. Later the route bears away from the watercourse and follows a hedge to bend left in front of buildings. Climb a stile by a gate onto a lane.

3. Turn left and in 20 yards cross a road and go right along the pavement over Cavendish Bridge with Shardlow Marina to your right. On your left pause at the memorial to the old Cavendish Bridge that was washed away in 1947 as it details an interesting scale of toll charges. Continuing into Shardlow, beyond the Navigation Inn and Broughton House on the opposite side of Wilne Lane – the home of the Sutton family before they later moved to Shardlow Hall – you return to the Trent and Mersey Canal.

4. Just before the canal bridge, turn left – signed Aston on Trent – onto a lane that offers views of the former wharf, including today's Clock Warehouse pub and the heritage centre. At the end of the wharf, by the Shardlow locks and former lock-keeper's house, turnaround and retrace your steps to the bridge, cross the road and drop back down onto the towpath. At the next bridge, beside two pubs, leave the waterway and turn right along Wilne Lane back to the car park.

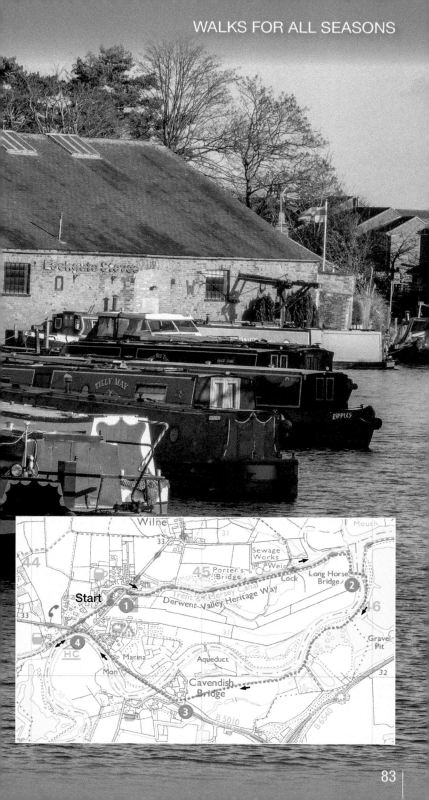

18 SHIPLEY COUNTRY PARK

EXPLORE THE WOODED PARKLAND, MEADOWS AND LAKES OF A 'SHIP-SHAPELY' COUNTRY PARK, WHICH WAS ONCE THE SEAT OF THE PROMINENT DERBYSHIRE MILLER-MUNDY FAMILY.

Don't let the approach to Shipley Country Park through an industrial estate put you off, as hidden beyond it is 700 acres of green and varied parkland laced with 20 miles of footpaths and a fine outlook across the wider countryside.

It's a scene that has witnessed many transformations. Recorded in the Domesday Book as a manor belonging to a nephew of William the Conqueror, during medieval times the Shipley estate was extensively forested and a highly prized hunting ground for the privileged few.

Over the centuries it passed through the hands of several notable families before landing in the coal sack of the Miller-Mundys in the early 18th century. The estate's owners had begun to strip the ground of its valuable fossil fuel from the 16th century, but it was the Miller-Mundys who took the extraction of this valuable resource to a different level, and from around 1765 they personally managed their own mining enterprise.

Unsurprisingly, this activity dramatically altered the landscape, as did the construction of the Nutbrook Canal and several associated water-supply reservoirs to provide a transport corridor to the Erewash Canal (Walk 10) and beyond to the Trent. In time, of course, the railway sidelined the canal.

The original Shipley Hall was built at the beginning of the 18th century, with substantial alterations being made thereafter as the Miller-Mundys' wealth rapidly accelerated, on a natural mound – Shipley Hill.

After the death of Alfred Miller-Mundy in 1920, the Shipley Colliery Company (formed by the Miller-Mundys) took over control of the mines through to nationalisation of the coal industry in 1947. In the end, the estate's principal source of income became its downfall, as the pillar of coal that the family dynasty had carefully left in place under their home was quickly pulled from under it by a new owner keen to capitalise on its business opportunity. The damage this caused later led to the hall being demolished.

After decades of neglect the estate was eventually purchased by Derbyshire County Council, who once again re-shaped the landscape into a country park that was opened in 1976 as a memorial to the local miners, with Shipley Hill as its centrepiece.

THE BASICS

Distance: 3¾ miles / 6km

Gradient: Gently undulating

Severity: Easy

Approx. time to walk: 2 hours

Stiles: None

Maps: OS Landranger 129 (Nottingham & Loughborough); OS Explorer 260 (Nottingham)

Path description: Good country park path, track and lane network

Start point: Shipley Country Park's Coppiceside car park, Slack Lane, Heanor (GR SK 431453)

Parking: Shipley Country Park's Coppiceside car park (charges apply), Slack Lane, Heanor (near DE75 7GX). Alternative parking at Mapperley Reservoir (DE75 6BR)

Dog friendly: Yes, under close control

Public toilets: Shipley Park's visitor centre and Derby Lodge tea rooms (at the time of walking the Mapperley Reservoir facilities were shut down due to vandalism)

Nearest food: Shipley Park's visitor centre cafe and Derby Lodge tea rooms

ROUTE

1. From the colliery wheel – in the parking area nearest the visitor centre – walk to a visitor centre signpost where there is a choice of three paths. Take the right-hand path to a junction. Turn left, soon passing the visitor centre and a private property, along a track. Go through a gap at the side of a gate and when the path splits branch left. The track bends left and then right, and you continue past Flatmeadow Farm to reach Bell Lane.

2. Turn right and shortly after the bridleway for Mapperley Reservoir, turn left onto an unsigned path into John Wood. At a T-junction, bear left over a footbridge and go left again at the next path intersection. Head right at the subsequent junction along the footpath that hugs the shoreline of Mapperley Reservoir to Shipley Lane.

3. Walk left along the lane and at a junction opposite the reservoir car park pick up the right-hand signed bridleway and follow this surfaced track, with extensive views to your left, past Home Farm to the Derby Lodge tea room.

4. Go right, and at a sign for the site of Shipley Hall you can make an optional detour, otherwise maintain direction by a wall on your right. At a fork, veer left down a bridleway – signed The Field – that later bends left. Join another track ahead through woodland to a lane next to the Lakeside Business Centre.

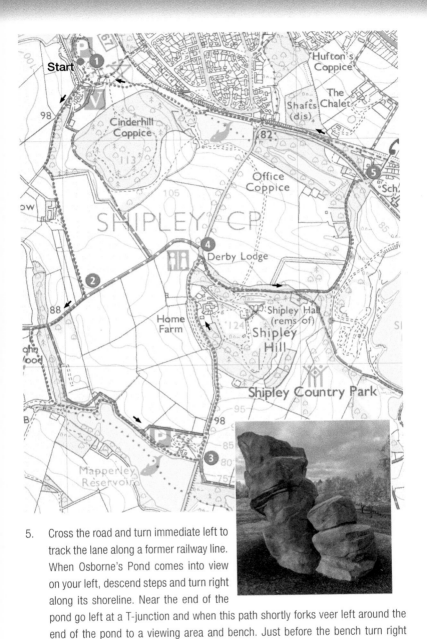

5. Cross the road and turn immediate left to track the lane along a former railway line. When Osborne's Pond comes into view on your left, descend steps and turn right along its shoreline. Near the end of the pond go left at a T-junction and when this path shortly forks veer left around the end of the pond to a viewing area and bench. Just before the bench turn right to gently ascend past a large gate to a crossroads and follow the car park sign slightly to the right to a T-junction. The colliery wheel is to your left.

19 SWARKESTONE

Unlike Bonnie Prince Charlie, you won't need to beat a hasty retreat at Swarkestone Bridge on the River Trent and can linger over the magnificence of England's longest stone bridge.

The Glorious Revolution of 1688 marked the end of the Catholic rule of James II when he was replaced by his Protestant daughter Mary and her husband, William of Orange. In 1715 James's son – the Old Pretender – led a failed uprising against Protestant George I. Then in 1745, the Old Pretender's son – popularly known as Bonnie Prince Charlie – set foot on British (Scottish) soil for the first time and also attempted to snatch the throne from the reigning monarch, George II.

Marching his army from the coast to Edinburgh, the Young Pretender swiftly captured Scotland. With London now on Charles's radar he headed south with his Jacobite – the name derived from the Latin name Jacobus for James – army to reclaim the throne for the Stuart dynasty. Unaware, however, of the panic this advance was causing in the capital, Charles lost his nerve on reaching the Swarkestone Bridge crossing of the Trent and fled back to Scotland.

In hot pursuit, the Hanoverians finally crushed the Jacobite rising at the decisive Battle of Culloden. Charles escaped from this defeat and with the help of the Scottish heroine Flora MacDonald, who disguised him as a woman, he made it to the Isle of Skye and on to France.

Swarkestone's 13th-century stone bridge and causeway, which majestically stretches for three quarters of a mile across the Trent, therefore symbolises one of the key turning points, quite literally, in British history. It's one of the great 'what ifs'.

Your route follows the north bank of the river from Barrow upon Trent to Swarkestone. Both these villages have a pleasing church and waterfront residences to admire. Also not to be missed is the 17th-century former coaching inn, now the Harpur & Crewe pub, with its long garden snuggled up to Swarkestone Bridge.

Leaving Swarkestone village behind, an isolated building comes into view. Sometimes referred to as a summerhouse, it was built by the Harpur family who lived at the one-time Swarkestone Hall. This was the principal seat of the Harpurs until they moved to Calke Abbey (Walk 5) and although its purpose is unknown it's probable that they used it to hold banquets and as a bowling alley.

Your return to Barrow upon Trent is along the Trent and Mersey Canal (more information is provided in Walk 17) and passes the popular Swarkestone Junction where the abandoned Derby canal connected into the main inland waterway network.

THE BASICS

Distance: 3½ miles / 5.5km

Gradient: Level throughout

Severity: Easy

Approx. time to walk: 1¾ hours

Stiles: Two

Maps: OS Landranger 128 (Derby & Burton upon Trent); OS Explorer 245 (National Forest)

Path description: Field paths, riverside, canal towpath and lanes. Fields beside River Trent liable to seasonal mud. Some busy roads to cross.

Start point: Barrow upon Trent village centre, off the A5132 (GR SK 353285)

Parking: Courteous roadside parking in Barrow upon Trent village centre, off the A5132 (DE73 7HG)

Dog friendly: Yes, but on leads for road sections

Public toilets: None

Nearest food: Crewe and Harpur pub next to Swarkestone Bridge at Swarkestone

ROUTE

1. From the village centre, follow Church Lane to St Wilfred's Church, where it bends left. When the lane ends maintain direction on a footpath beside the River Trent. Cross a footbridge and follow field edges alongside the river with Swarkestone Bridge later coming into sight. Turn right at a lane to soon meet the A514 in between the Crewe & Harpur pub and Swarkestone Bridge.

2. Cross the road and rejoin the riverbank. If you turnaround there are good views of the river and Swarkestone Bridge. When the track reaches a lane, walk left to St James's Church. Immediately after the church, bear right across a grassy area for 20 yards and climb a stile into a field. The summerhouse to the former Swarkestone Hall is to your right. Head diagonally right across the field to climb a stile onto the A5132.

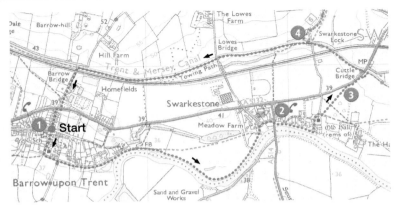

3. Go right along the pavement and in 100 yards, just after crossing Cuttle Brook, fork right at a signpost down to the Trent and Mersey canal towpath. Walk left – signed Derby – under a railway bridge to Swarkestone Lock and the barges moored at the Swarkestone Junction with the disused Derby canal.

4. Continue along the towpath under Lowes Bridge to Barrow Bridge. Here leave the canal and walk left along Sinfin Lane, go over the railway line and carefully cross the A5132 back into Barrow upon Trent village.

20 WIRKSWORTH

DELIGHT IN THE HIGGLEDY-PIGGLEDY CHARACTER OF THE SMALL TOWN OF WIRKSWORTH AND FEEL ON TOP OF THE WORLD AS YOU PUFF UP THE HIGH PEAK TRAIL'S MIDDLETON INCLINE TO THE LANDMARK MIDDLETON TOP ENGINE HOUSE.

Standing virtually at the centre of Derbyshire, the market town of Wirksworth rose to prosperity as a significant centre for lead mining. Such activity dates back to at least the Romans, and in 1288 Wirksworth established the Barmote Court to enforce local mining laws, which incredibly still sits twice a year today at its Moot Hall. The industry reached its zenith between 1600 and 1780, before eventually falling into decline at the end of the 19th century.

Fortunately, from the perspective of the town's workers, limestone quarrying, which again has local roots in ancient times, became a major enterprise for Wirksworth between the 1860s and 1980s.

Your route heads north from Wirksworth to the National Stone Centre (free admission). This 50-acre site set within six former limestone quarries guides you through the history of stone and includes a series of trails.

You then join the High Peak Trail, that runs for 17½ miles (27km) from the High Peak Junction on the Cromford Canal to Parsley Hay. Built in 1829, this early railway – the Cromford and High Peak – was an engineering masterpiece based on canal principles, with inclines acting as a substitution for locks, to traverse the landscape. Astonishingly the line remained in use until 1963.

Nowadays only three of the original nine inclines of the track remain, but such was the severity of the gradients that the wagons had to be raised, or lowered, along each slope by a steam-driven winding engine. The sole survivor of these engine houses is at Middleton Top, which serviced the 1-in-8 gradient of the Middleton Incline. It is now in the care of Derbyshire County Council, and you can stop off at the visitor centre or see the restored engine in action at occasional demonstrations throughout the year.

Shortly after Middleton Top you leave the High Peak Trail to cross fields and link into a well-protected track through one-time limestone quarry workings. You get a sense of the enormous scale of this operation, and impressive views across the Ecclesbourne Valley, from Stoney Wood.

Perched above Wirksworth, Stoney Wood was a proud Millennium community project, which later added the *Star Disc* sculpture. This 21st-century stone circle depicts the northern hemisphere's night sky. Twelve seats around its perimeter represent the months of the year. Powered by our nearest star, the sun, low-level lighting illuminates the *Star Disc* during the hours of darkness.

Dropping steeply down into Wirksworth you can explore the Market Place and its surrounding jumble of buildings, yards, alleys and narrow streets. A new heritage centre is due to open in mid-2018.

THE BASICS

Distance: 3 miles / 4.8km

Gradient: Although this route is a little more challenging than usual, it's fairly short and has plenty of interest breaks along the way. From the start a gentle track ascends to the National Stone Centre. This is followed by a more severe ascent of the High Peak Trail's Middleton Incline. Then an undulating track traverses a former quarry, and finally a steep lane drops you into the centre of Wirksworth.

Severity: Moderate

Approx. time to walk: 2 hours

Stiles: One

Maps: OS Landranger 119 (Buxton & Matlock); OS Explorer OL24 (The Peak District – White Peak Area)

Path description: Multi-user High Peak Trail, field paths and good tracks. Care with children and dogs is required around former quarries.

Start point: Old Lane car park off the B5036 to the north of Wirksworth town centre (GR SK 286545)

Parking: Old Lane car park (free) off the B5036 to the north of Wirksworth town centre (DE4 4FP). Free parking – donations appreciated at the honesty box – is also available at the National Stone Centre (DE4 4LS). There are various pay car parks around Wirksworth town centre and one at Middleton Top engine house (also near DE4 4LS).

Dog friendly: Yes, but preferably on leads around old quarry workings

Public toilets: National Stone Centre visitor centre, Middleton Top visitor centre and Wirksworth town centre (signed)

Nearest food: National Stone Centre cafe and various in Wirksworth town centre. Seasonal snacks are also available at Middleton Top.

20 WIRKSWORTH WALK

ROUTE

1. Exit the car park entrance and turn left along Old Lane, which immediately becomes a rough track. Steadily climb this track, ignoring all side paths, to pass under a railway bridge and enter the National Stone Centre by an information board, later reaching its visitor centre.

2. When you are ready, continue past this modern building along a surfaced lane. Just before a railway bridge in 40 yards bear right at a marker post up to the High Peak Trail. Turn left along the trail – signed Middleton Top – with a panorama to your left over  Wirksworth. After passing the Wheel Pit you begin a stiff climb up the Middleton Incline. Take a breather part way up to admire views to your right across the Derwent Valley towards Matlock and the mock Gothic Riber Castle sat on a hill overlooking the town. At the top of the slope is the Middleton Top engine house.

3. After the engine house stay on the High Peak Trail for several hundred yards to a gate. Go left – signed Wirksworth – onto a track. In 15 yards turn right at a signpost and drop down to a gate into a field. Maintain direction to a wall corner and then walk with a wall on your left. Pass through a gap and head across the middle of two fields to the B5035.

4. Cross the road and climb a stile into a field. Continue forwards over two fields and in the third field bear right to walk by a wall protecting a quarry to a gate. Go through the gate and walk along a rolling wire-fenced track across former quarry workings, heeding the numerous warnings about the dangers beyond the secure fencing.

5. On meeting a lane on a bend veer left, stopping off at Stoney Wood – you can't miss its elaborate entrance in 75 yards – to admire the vistas and the *Star Disc* artwork. Continue along the lane, which descends very steeply through quaint Wirksworth to its Market Place on the town's main  road. Turn left along the pavement heading under a bridge and past a school and crematorium on your right back to the Old Lane car park.

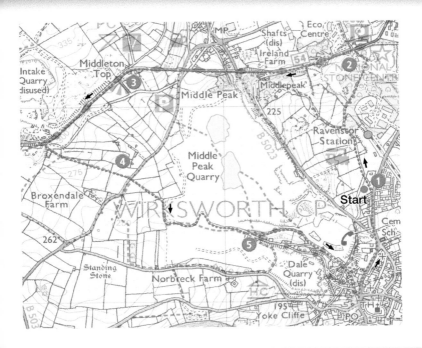

ABOUT THE AUTHOR

Carol Burkinshaw has lived close to the Derbyshire border all of her life and as a keen walker is, as you'd expect, a regular visitor to the glorious Peak District national park, of which Derbyshire forms a sizeable chunk.

At busy times, however, the national park's honeypots are heaving with people and Carol loves to escape the crowds and ferret out great walks in the quieter parts of this diverse county.

With the benefit of hindsight, Carol admits she had been missing a trick that was right on her doorstep for years. 'Off Peak' Derbyshire, she says, has so much to offer to all, but is particularly suitable for families and friends seeking gentler outings throughout the seasons.

Over the past twenty years, Carol has roamed far and wide across Europe bringing her travel experiences of top destinations and secret hideaways to life through articles published in national magazines, which she illustrates with her own photography.

Walking, however, is Carol's true passion and the driving force behind her work. She regularly contributes rambling routes from across the country to a major walking magazine. And she has stepped out previously into Derbyshire, along with Nottinghamshire and her native South Yorkshire (*Walks For All Ages – South Yorkshire* is published by Bradwell Books) to produce some in-depth regional walking guidebooks.

But Carol now feels the time is right to lift off the invisibility cloak of an underappreciated part of Derbyshire bursting with alluring vistas, teeming with wildlife and dripping in heritage – a more domesticated 'Great Outdoors'.